PENGUIN BOOKS

On Reading
The Grapes of Wrath

SUSAN SHILLINGLAW is a professor of English at San Jose State University and scholar in residence at the National Steinbeck Center in Salinas, California. For eighteen years she was director of the Center for Steinbeck Studies at SJSU, and she received the 2012–2013 SJSU President's Scholar Award. She is the author of *Carol and John Steinbeck: Portrait of a Marriage* and *A Journey into Steinbeck's California,* and has edited several Steinbeck volumes. For Penguin Classics, she has written introductions to *The Portable Steinbeck, Of Mice and Men, Cannery Row, A Russian Journal, The Winter of Our Discontent,* and *"America and Americans" and Selected Nonfiction,* which she also coedited.

ON READING
THE GRAPES
OF WRATH

• • •

SUSAN SHILLINGLAW

PENGUIN BOOKS

PENGUIN BOOKS
Published by the Penguin Group
Penguin Group (USA) LLC
375 Hudson Street
New York, New York 10014

USA | Canada | UK | Ireland | Australia
New Zealand | India | South Africa | China
penguin.com
A Penguin Random House Company

First published in Penguin Books 2014

LIBRARY OF CONGRESS CATALOGING-IN-PUBLICATION DATA
Shillinglaw, Susan, author.
On Reading the Grapes of Wrath / Susan Shillinglaw.
pages cm
Includes bibliographical references.
ISBN 978-0-14-312550-1 (pbk.)
1. Steinbeck, John, 1902–1968. Grapes of wrath. 2. Steinbeck, John,
1902–1968—Influence. I. Title.
PS3537.T3234G888 2014
813'.52—dc23   2013042937

Printed in the United States of America
1 3 5 7 9 10 8 6 4 2

Set in Adobe Garamond Pro
Designed by Elke Sigal

CONTENTS

Preface ix

A Note on the Text xv

On Reading *The Grapes of Wrath* xvii

CHAPTER 1   New Start Big Writing   1

CHAPTER 2   Five Layers   8

CHAPTER 3   "Stay with the detail."   14

CHAPTER 4   Scientist and Writer   25

CHAPTER 5   A Journal, the Turtle, and Interchapters   31

CHAPTER 6   Participation   39

CHAPTER 7   This "Middlebrow" Book   45

CHAPTER 8   Isolatoes and the Greater Whole   53

CHAPTER 9   Wrath   60

CHAPTER 10   Woman to Woman   66

CHAPTER 11   Pictures   73

CHAPTER 12   "Loose Aggregations"   81

CHAPTER 13   The Salinas Lettuce Strike, 1936   87

CHAPTER 14   History on the Outside   94

CHAPTER 15   "They's a lot a fellas wanta know
what reds is."   102

CHAPTER 16   History on the Inside   108

CHAPTER 17   Migrants   114

CHAPTER 18   "Care like hell."   117

CHAPTER 19   Beyond the Joad Niche   127

CHAPTER 20   Systemic Sins   139

CHAPTER 21   Ma to Tom: "Ever'thing you do is
more'n you."   143

CHAPTER 22   Ricketts on *Grapes*   150

CHAPTER 23   The Book   154

CHAPTER 24   Reactions   165

CHAPTER 25   Did *The Grapes of Wrath* Help
the Migrants?   172

CHAPTER 26   The Film   176

CHAPTER 27   "None of it is important or
all of it is."   181

Notes   187

Bibliography   203

Preface

◆ ◆ ◆

Anniversaries help us reconsider. When *The Grapes of Wrath* marked its golden year, in 1989, the television program *Sunday Morning*, gracefully moderated by Charles Kuralt, aired a segment on the novel. It begins with the author's son John IV reading the opening paragraph, the camera cutting between his reading, clips of the Dust Bowl, and rain falling on Steinbeck's statue in front of the John Steinbeck Library in Salinas, California, the author's hometown. While the opening segment is intimate and familial, the closing scene of this program is broad and urgent. It ends with Tom Joad's final speech to Ma, Henry Fonda's words (from the 1940 film of *Grapes*) laid over clips of the homeless in New York City, the fall of the Berlin Wall, and the angry student protesters in Tiananmen Square. I have replayed this many times for classes. Each time I tear up because it makes Steinbeck's words so urgent and essential for a compassionate world.

Steinbeck wanted that kind of reaction, I'm sure, since it's only when we feel deeply about something—human rights, immigration reform, gun control—that things finally happen. Tom Joad's single paragraph exit from the novel is an impassioned plea for connection with other humans and participation in an agitated world. Care about the woe of others, as Tom promises to do, and then, perhaps, something will happen.

Tom isn't a reformer. He has no answers, no solutions to any one social problem. His speech unrolls as a series of pictures, rough outlines whose details are to be filled in fifty and seventy-five and one hundred years after the book's publication: "Wherever they's a fight so hungry people can eat, I'll be there. Wherever they's a cop beatin' up a guy, I'll be there." The reader supplies the particulars, and our history since the 1939 publication of *The Grapes of Wrath* has given us many scenes that are sadly appropriate: the public space of China's Tiananmen Square has become Egypt's Tahrir or Turkey's Taksim; the fall of the Berlin Wall has become the Arab Spring. And 1989's repossessed farms have become repossessed homes a quarter century later. Reviewing the fiftieth anniversary edition of the novel, the author William Kennedy said that this book is a "vivid 50-year-old parallel to the American homeless: a story of people at the bottom of the world, bereft and drifting outcasts in a hostile society." And while migrant housing has steadily improved throughout California and elsewhere, the homeless remain on the streets of cities and towns, camping in forest retreats.

Another picture, replicated throughout history. On May 19, 2013, the *New York Times* ran an article on Syria by Thomas Friedman, "Without Water, Revolution." The mix of contributing factors in Syria's conflict is eerily familiar: starting in 2000, "big farmers" were allowed to buy up land and drill for unlimited water, thus diminishing the water table; small farmers started abandoning their dry land for the towns and cities (in some towns, populations swelled from 2,000 to 400,000 people in a decade); and an "extreme weather event," drought, between 2006 and 2011 accelerated the exodus. And that lethal ecological mix helped to fuel a rebellion. In effect, the Syrian picture seems not unlike the story of 1930s croppers in Dust Bowl Oklahoma at the mercy of California agribusiness, but without a sympathetic government (in Syria).

The Grapes of Wrath is a novel that won't be contained by its setting, the 1930s. Certainly it's *about* a particular time and place and people—the Oklahoma migrants who made their way ever so slowly to California, imagining a new start in the state of orange groves and verdant fields. And there is urgency in the particularity of that moment. Steinbeck is at his best in helping us see clearly the diaspora of Dust Bowl migrants in the 1930s: the pork they salt and clothes they wear; the dust that covers the houses they leave and the rules that govern the camps they create along the way; and the steady, crawling movement along U.S. Highway 66. But everywhere in this book, starting with the biblical cadence of the opening chapter, Steinbeck nudges readers out of the 1930s into the timeless and the mythic. The Joads themselves would not have seen their flight from Oklahoma to California as an Exodus to a promised land. They would not have seen themselves as latter-day everymen, trudging to a world of possibility, or on an odyssey to find home.

Tom Joad would not have compared himself to Joe Hill, labor organizer, or to Christ, committed to the meek. But Steinbeck did. He suggests all these parallels, and in so doing lifts dispossession and yearning for a decent life from one time to all time. The Joads become the Syrians huddling near Turkish or Lebanese borders, or Mexicans reaching hands through fences at America's border, or the hungry, the jobless, and the exiled everywhere.

Let me suggest the power of this book by quoting from Steinbeck's next, a kind of intertextual urgency that is, I think, appropriate when reading *The Grapes of Wrath* in the twenty-first century, when we inhabit an ever more fragile global ecosystem. Both *The Grapes of Wrath* and *Sea of Cortez* (1941) are ecological texts, the latter a meditation on much that Steinbeck thought during the 1930s. Both books consider the interconnections between humans and their environment—environment understood to mean not simply nature but other species, human and natural histories, and the spiritual vibration of place. The two books form a diptych, two journeys of discovery, one fiction, one nonfiction; two meditations on humans living in place, connected to land, to animals, and to one another. *Sea of Cortez* begins with this reflection about the interconnectedness of life, one of my favorite passages in all of Steinbeck:

> We take a tiny colony of soft corals from a rock in a little water world. And that isn't terribly important to the tide pool. Fifty miles away the Japanese shrimp boats are dredging with overlapping scoops, bringing up tons of shrimps, rapidly de-

stroying the species so that it may never come back, and with the species destroying the ecological balance of the whole region. That isn't very important in the world. And thousands of miles away the great bombs are falling on London and the stars are not moved thereby. None of it is important or all of it is.

For ethical living, that might profitably be read daily by anyone. *The Grapes of Wrath* amplifies that insistent holistic truth: individuals belong to families, blood families are bound to other family units, and all humans are connected in spirit. The structure of this novel also replicates that passage, moving from particular to general—rocking back and forth between the intimate Joad narrative and the expansive interchapters that give documentary and historical heft to the misery and endurance of one family. Small gestures and cataclysmic events are equally important in imperiled times, true when *Grapes* was published in 1939, true when *Sea of Cortez* was published in December 1941, and true today. In *The Grapes of Wrath* Steinbeck placed the Joads' particular sorrows in the context of a much larger migrant exodus from the Southwest to California.

We come back to this novel because the Joad family plight as well as the generalized migrant woe revealed in the interchapters fold into even larger stories, both national and international: dispossession, power, land use, the interconnections of humans and other species, the suffering of many who can't tell their own story.

And we come back to this book because Steinbeck

asks us to open our hearts: "And here's a story you can hardly believe, but it's true," he writes in one interchapter, recounting the tale of a family of twelve forced off their land: They built a trailer—they couldn't afford a car—and hauled it to the side of Route 66 and waited. A man in a sedan stopped, hitched up the trailer, and pulled it all the way to California, five of the family riding with him in the car, seven in the trailer. How did that family by the side of the road have faith that someone would pick them up? the authorial voice asks. "Very few things would teach us such faith."

It's a haunting thought. Steinbeck brings readers to such faith, faith in our own species.

A Note on the Text

◆ ◆ ◆

This is, in effect, a cooperative reading of *The Grapes of Wrath*, looking at how the relationship between Steinbeck and his closest friend, Edward F. Ricketts, a marine biologist, shaped this novel of displaced peoples, their habitats, and their great spirit—tracing connections that we now call deep ecology. The structure of this little book loosely imitates Steinbeck's novel, with its alternating narrative chapters about the Joad family and interchapters or intercalary chapters that broaden the picture of migrant woe. *On Reading "The Grapes of Wrath"* considers Steinbeck's text as well as cultural and biographical contexts in roughly alternating chapters.

The organizing principle of this book is also guided by Steinbeck's notion of five layers, as I move from layer one (detail, plot, characters) through five (emergent life).

There are some plot spoilers here, especially near the end, although Steinbeck's great book is concerned with life itself, not resolution. The best way to approach *On Reading "The Grapes of Wrath,"* perhaps, is to dip in, read *Grapes*, and dip back.

This book would not exist without the support of three women: Colleen Bailey, the director of the National Steinbeck Center, who invited me to accompany her on a trip to New York City to plan seventy-fifth-anniversary outreach; Elda Rotor, the associate publisher and editorial director of Penguin Classics, who asked me to write the book—and believed that I could do so in two-plus months; and Joanne O'Hare, the director of the University of Nevada Press, who gave permission to reprint material on "The Harvest Gypsies" from my biography *Carol and John Steinbeck: Portrait of a Marriage* (2013) and encouraged me to "go for it," a great boost. My sincere thanks to each.

On Reading

The Grapes of Wrath

◆ ◆ ◆

CHAPTER I

NEW START BIG WRITING

◆ ◆ ◆

IN MAY 1938, John Steinbeck sat down to write the final draft of the book he had been researching for nearly three years. At the top of the first page he wrote boldly, "New Start Big Writing." He was reminding himself to write legibly so that his wife, Carol, who typed and edited all of his manuscripts, could read his famously minuscule scrawl. But his writing got smaller and smaller as he knuckled down to work, pen in hand.

The tools of his trade were of vital concern to Steinbeck, a man whose calling—whose passion—was words, from about age fourteen to the end of his life. He wrote both in pen and in pencil, depending on the decade, depending on his mood. Early in his career, he favored a pen. His first novel, *Cup of Gold* (1929), written and rewritten in a Lake Tahoe cabin in 1927 and 1928, was a historical romance about Henry Morgan, privateer, pirate, and seeker: "I have taken to writing with a steel pen," he wrote home to his parents in Salinas, California. "I do my first draft with a pen, you know." For the next decade or so he continued that practice. "What an extension of self is this pen," he mused as he was about to begin writing *Of Mice and Men* in 1936. "Once it is in my hand like a wand, I stop being the confused, turgid, ugly and gross person. I am no longer the me I know. Very dear pen." The paper he used, however, had less to do with choice than necessity. Since he and Carol had so little money in the early 1930s, he composed stories in his father's discarded ledger books, "half full" of his father's figures. (Mr. Steinbeck was treasurer of Monterey County and allowed the young couple to live rent-free in the family's summer cottage in Pacific Grove, California.) Once, John used purple ink since it was on sale at a local department store.

By the time he sat down to write *The Grapes of Wrath*, thirty-six-year-old John Steinbeck could afford a house of his own, better pens, and paper of his own choosing. For his "big book" he used an oversized ledger book purchased the year before in a San Jose bookstore, "a thirteen dollar ledger for a dollar . . . thick enough for ten years' work and the most wonderful paper in the world. I gloat," he wrote a friend. "The great ledger" he would call it, ten by sixteen inches.

Later in his career he became a "pencil fiend," admitting to one friend that he used "pencils like butter." In 1950, he experimented with graphite ones, no wood, that were "[m]ade in Czeckoslovakia (how the hell do you spell it?). . . . That is one fine thing about my trade," he concluded. "The equipment is very slight. . . . All in the world I need are yellow pads and pencils."

This writer cared not only about pencils and pens, but also, as any reader of his novels knows, about other things he held in his hands: a hoe, a gun, tools. He was a gardener and, when young, a hunter of quail and squirrels and rabbits. He was a wood-carver, a tinker, and an inventor. In the living room of the Los Gatos house where he wrote *The Grapes of Wrath* was a fireplace covered with a conical copper hood of his own design.

When you read the detailed description of Tom Joad skinning a rabbit for his meal with Casy and Muley, you know that Steinbeck, as a boy in the Salinas Valley, skinned his own rabbits. There's authority in the description, as there is in Tom taking the oil pan off the Wilsons' touring car, "loosening the bolts with a wrench and turning them out with his fingers," later cutting his hand: "I never fixed no car in my life 'thout cuttin' myself."

In *The Grapes of Wrath* people use tools and work with their hands: the Joads salt down a hog, cook stew and cornmeal mush, dig ditches, patch tires, pick peaches and cotton and throw mud on a levee to contain floodwaters. Others pump gas, wipe down a café counter, fry hamburgers. Everyone works with his or her hands—except the questioning man, Casy, who admits he has no idea how to fix a car. Old Tom Joad is hammering when Tom comes home, Ma is cooking, "lifting the curling slices of pork from the frying pan." Her hands are "white with flour" when she makes gravy; they are as "sure and cool and quiet" as a healer. Tom has "hard" hands, and the "space between thumb and forefinger and the hams of his hands were shiny with callus." As the truck driver who picks Tom up in chapter 2 notes, Tom has been "swingin' a pick or an ax or a sledge. That shines up your hands." Tom is a "first-grade muckstick man," Wilkie Wallace says as Tom digs a ditch. Laboring hands are texts in this novel, telling life stories.

Clasped in her lap, Ma's hands rest "like tired lovers," her spirit exhausted. When she's angry, a hand grasps a jack handle, later a skillet when a cop calls her an Okie: "In my country you watch your tongue," she tells him. Hands hold emotion, the patience and fury of mother love, so central to this family saga.

A student once asked me how Al Joad would know anything about television in 1938. As Steinbeck undoubtedly knew, experiments in television broadcasts had been ongoing for a decade; the 1939 Golden Gate International Exposition in San Francisco featured television. For Al to want to study this new technology signaled his motivation—a goal that was something like wanting to search for life on Europa today. Al is clever and innovative and cagey, edgy and restless. He's also good with his hands, an adaptable and visionary worker.

Steinbeck's indispensable tool was not a hoe or a wrench but a pen or a pencil. A scribe of the worker, he empathized with the powerless and knew something about manual labor himself. Born in 1902 in Salinas, a prosperous town in one of California's most productive agricultural regions, John Steinbeck saw migrant workers in the fields, turning ground for sugar beets, when he was a child. At the nearby Spreckels Sugar plant, he worked as a bench chemist, side by side with Mexican laborers when he was in high school. He worked on a dredging crew near Castroville, now an artichoke region, draining water from swamps so that more crops could be planted. Briefly he joined a construction crew building U.S. Highway 1 that connects the Monterey Peninsula to Big Sur. After a few listless quarters attending Stanford University, he dropped out to work for Spreckels on several ranches around California.

Growing up feeling like an outsider in respectable Salinas, Steinbeck sympathized with others like himself— those who were shunned, those on the lower rungs who worked with their hands. Chinese, Japanese, Filipino, and Mexican field-workers were brought to the Salinas Valley in successive waves from the mid–nineteenth century on to thrash wheat and barley, to hoe sugar beets, then to pick lettuce, which, in the twentieth century, became the "green gold" of the valley. One of Steinbeck's earliest stories, published in the *Stanford Spectator*, was called "Fingers of Cloud," about a dreamy young girl who ends up in a Filipino work camp. Another story written while he was at Stanford is about a lonely ranch blacksmith, snubbed by the workers. Although John Steinbeck was middle class by birth and by education, he was drawn to working-class experiences by his own feelings of cultural displacement.

Steinbeck's own work defined him. "Writing is a sort of nervous tic with me," he told a reporter in 1963. "I would go crazy if I didn't write." Nearly every day of his life he wrote letters or journal entries to warm up, then fiction or nonfiction, short essays or plays or film scripts. "Much of what I write, I throw away," he admitted. "In all of my books, with the exception of *East of Eden*, what is published represents about one-fifth of what I actually wrote." Before he sat down to compose *The Grapes of Wrath* in May 1938, he had scribbled notes and scenes for over two years, most crumpled. But in the five months of writing the final version, he was monomaniacal, as he admitted to his agent, consumed and exhausted by words, which got smaller and smaller as he turned the pages of his great ledger: "[T]he small writing has always intrigued me. It is amazing what a difference the small writing makes to the type of mss. It causes a kind of concentration that big writing does not," he wrote in a later journal.

On the opening page of the *Grapes* manuscript, as Roy Simmonds notes in "The Original Manuscript," Steinbeck wrote 648 words in Big Writing. By page 19, there are 886 words on the page. He started writing in the margins, skipped paragraphs, omitted punctuation. On page 71 there are 1,081 words and by page 156 there are 1,319 words. Steinbeck's pen scratched on overdrive.

Midway through writing this little book, I went to the Oregon Shakespeare Festival in Ashland, Oregon, and saw *King Lear*. The program notes from the director, Bill Rauch, who is also the artistic director at Ashland, resonated. Rauch writes:

> One of my all-time favorite lines is in *King Lear*. The storm rages. The single most privileged man in his society encounters his almost-naked god-

son in disguise. And how does the former king describe a mentally challenged homeless person groveling in the mud? "Thou art the thing itself."

The thing itself: Shakespeare's achievement in *King Lear* and, it seems to me, Steinbeck's in *The Grapes of Wrath*. The human condition, stripped down, dispossessed, can be a thing of wonder—resilient people, defined by the tools of their work.

There is great dignity in labor, in working with your hands, as Steinbeck's book reminds us.

CHAPTER 2

FIVE LAYERS

◆ ◆ ◆

IN MID-JANUARY 1939, three months before publication of *The Grapes of Wrath*, Steinbeck wrote a long letter to his editor at Viking Press, Pascal (Pat) Covici. He wanted Covici, in particular, to understand this book, to appreciate what he was up to. And so he concluded with a statement that might serve as a preface in and of itself:

> Throughout I've tried to make the reader participate in the actuality, what he takes from it will be scaled entirely on his own depth or shallowness. There are five layers in this book, a reader will find as many as he can and he wont find more than he has in himself.

The notion of layers undoubtedly came about through conversations with marine biologist Ed Ricketts, with whom Steinbeck shared a friendship almost unearthly in its intensity. For eighteen years, from 1930 to 1948, the two men were comrades of the spirit. Theirs was a life-altering attachment, each nurturing the other. (Consider, as a pale shadow of its intensity, Tom's relationship with Casy. In Steinbeck's fiction, male friendship is always the most nuanced human bond.) Ricketts admired Steinbeck's single-minded devotion to writing, and Steinbeck appreciated Ricketts's scientific expertise and philosophical curiosity. Ricketts's mind, Steinbeck wrote later, had "no horizons." They "sparked one another," said a friend.

The intellectual and emotional bond between writer and scientist—a platonic love—was so unusual, so forward-looking, and so fiercely linked to a holistic understanding of humans and the environment that to see one is to see both and to understand both is to reconsider our own footprint in the world.

Behind the structure of *The Grapes of Wrath* lie Ricketts's observations on "four approaches" to ecology, how "basic principles" and methods of studying ecology become increasingly complex, layer by layer. Although Ricketts wrote out these ideas in 1945, he and Steinbeck discussed them throughout the 1930s, when the notion of ecology was rarely considered by scientists. Much of Ricketts's earlier writing makes it clear that ecological holism was at the base of all of his thought. "Ecology is the science of relationships," Ricketts writes, and the "value of building, of trying to build, whole pictures. . . . An ecologist has to consider the parts, each in its place, and as related to, rather than as subsidiary to, the whole."

The Grapes of Wrath considers the ecology of human

relationships, layer by layer, with an ever more complex appreciation of the intricate ties that bind humans to one another and to their habitats and histories.

For both writer and scientist, understanding begins with the most obvious things. The first approach to studying ecology for Ricketts was cataloguing the "little beasties," as he termed the invertebrate animals he observed with delight, "with regard to the environment." The first approach to reading *The Grapes of Wrath* is similar. Steinbeck considers the migrants' habits and behaviors and houses and food and clothes—the detailed connection of humans to place. Layer one.

Ricketts's second method of ecological awareness—a deeper appreciation—considers interactions among species, noting connections, the "loose aggregations of several species, or associations, into which animals band themselves." Migrants bond in the novel, and *The Grapes of Wrath* moves steadily from "I" to "we" and from the family unit to the family of man.

These two layers are the groundwork of the book: setting, character, and action. Beyond that are others.

Ricketts's third method of ecological understanding considers life histories: "If you know the natural history, but especially the complete life history of the beasts chiefly involved, you can allocate it [the presence of a particular animal] accurately and understand just how and even why it occurs in a certain place at a given period in its life history—to what association or associations it belongs at various times of its life, and why." Woven into the fabric of this novel are histories of farming on the Great Plains, bank consolidation, the Dust Bowl, California agriculture, the Associated Farmers, and the government migrant camp program in California, and all of these histories deepen readers' appreciation of the Joads' story. Layer three.

Ricketts's fourth "significant method hasn't even been suggested so far as I know," he wrote—a reminder of how groundbreaking the study of ecology was in the 1930s and 1940s. Ecological niches, Ricketts suggested, are basically equivalent in different regions. Intertidal animals occupy similar niches in different parts of the world, even though they often represent species that are not at all closely related. This fourth layer of understanding ecology thus underlies universal principles. Similarly, the Joads' niche—dispossessed Oklahomans—is hardly confined to one era, one family, or one habitat. Steinbeck's fourth layer takes readers to universals: cross-cultural, cross-historical accounts of land use, dispossession, and exile. The Joads' story stretches across place and time. Mythic stories shadow the novel: the biblical Exodus, Christ's sacrifice, *The Odyssey*, Bunyan's *Pilgrim's Progress*, as well as America's westering pioneers and the Cherokee Indians' "Trail of Tears" into Oklahoma, which took place exactly a century before Steinbeck wrote *The Grapes of Wrath*. Dispossession has many niches, mythic and historical.

Emergence is the fifth layer, which is not part of Ricketts's ecological schema but is intimately a part of his broader thinking—the belief that humans could "break through" to a larger, broader, spiritual, all-encompassing awareness. For Ed Ricketts, it was "the same thing that Jung has in mind when he discusses the 5th or emergent psychic function. To which thinking, feeling, intuition and sensation all contribute, and in which they all merge. A super intuition. The junction of Swedenborg's divine love and divine wisdom. The result of what I call 'breaking through.'" In *The Grapes of Wrath*, emergence is psychic and historical growth, human possibility, the burgeoning of life itself from innumerable interactions. It was an idea Steinbeck had grappled with for several years: "Out here" in the west, Steinbeck wrote to a friend in 1934, "with some distance between for the sight to get clean of effect, it is clearly visible that the old life is dying very rapidly, that a period of terror, of the cruelty and savage horror man creates when he is trying to get straight on something, is immanent." What *might* emerge is suggested again and again in this book: "Ever'thing we do—seems to me is aimed right at goin' on," Ma tells Pa and Uncle John late in the novel.

"There are five layers in this book, a reader will find as many as he can and he wont find more than he has in himself." With that, Steinbeck sent editor and future readers sleuthing for layers.

Of course I bring my own "warp" (Steinbeck's term) to this reading of *The Grapes of Wrath*, one that bends to the ecological, as did Steinbeck's, not only in the 1930s, when he and Ricketts were close, but for the whole of his career. (The structure of his last published book, *America and Americans* [1966], mimics Ricketts's methods: Steinbeck catalogued the American people as Ricketts catalogued intertidal animals, and his investigation of our national character moves through layers of complexity. Americans "are a very curious people and as far as I know no one has inspected us as we would inspect some other sub-species.")

Other readers with a different warp may identify Steinbeck's five layers in *The Grapes of Wrath* in other ways, and that is how it should be. The greatest books open up in many directions. If it were not so, this novel would not enjoy a hearty seventy-fifth anniversary, a centennial to come.

CHAPTER 3

"STAY WITH THE DETAIL."

◆ ◆ ◆

OBSERVATION IS THE first principle of field studies. A marine educator told my stunned class that his dissertation adviser would not allow students to choose a thesis topic until they had spent a year simply looking at invertebrate animals in the intertidal.

At low tide, that educator took twenty-five participants from the National Endowment for the Humanities' Steinbeck Institute into the intertidal of Monterey Bay, where each high school teacher selected one animal to study for a happy hour. Two years after his intertidal adventure, a participant from Oregon sent me this energetic e-mail: "What great fun that was—my memorable adventure with the anemone and the hermit crab barges into my thoughts regularly, sometimes like previews of a comedy adventure with maybe jim belushi and sandra bullock, sometimes like a hybrid of an old black and white horror flick with lon chaney in the male lead and madeline kahn providing the balancing levity . . . other times a pensive and reflective and painful love story gone awry like kramer vs kramer, only without the little kid . . . the battle I witnessed . . . stays with me and always represents something deeper than the mere battle for survival in the intertidal." A 2013 institute participant posted a sea hare video on YouTube; he channeled Jacques Cousteau's voice and intoned that the sea hare is "beautiful, majestic, looks like a moving kidney." Steady observation is transformative. "Stay low and go slow" is a phrase the NEH high school teachers remember.

Steinbeck asks his readers to go through the same process, or nearly. Consider the benefits of full participation—seeing, hearing, smelling, touching. Understanding starts there.

Details matter in *The Grapes of Wrath*. New grass and a bayonet of green. Tom Joad's yellow shoes. A feeny bush. IITYWYBAD?, a bar sign on a card "picked out with shining mica." Details niggle at readers, linger: "Who wears yellow shoes?" my husband wonders. And what the heck is a feeny bush? Indeed. As Steinbeck began the final draft of his novel about the lives of California migrants, his wife Carol's advice rolled through his mind: "Stay with the detail." And that refrain is one reason, one very good reason, to read and reread Steinbeck's most compelling novel. Figure out yellow shoes.

Details are the grace notes of Steinbeck's prose, as essential to his stories as are setting and character.

Much later in life, Steinbeck admitted to his editor, Pat Covici, that he had to begin with small and suggestive things, not the big picture. Steinbeck's first extant note about *Grapes*, written in the fall of 1936, is a snap-shot of place: "dust storm and the wind and the scouring of the land. And then the quiet . . . and the dust piled up like little snow drifts." That picture becomes the "scarred earth" of chapter 1, a wasteland created by man's plows that crossed and recrossed the rivulet marks, ignoring contours of the land. The first two sentences of this novel suggest that ecological destruction and human agency are connected. The eye then catches details of the land itself, a throbbing red sun, wilting weeds. The first chapter is a ground's-eye view of the Dust Bowl. Years of drought, thousands of acres long planted in a single crop (cotton in the novel), and the misery that gripped a clutch of states across the Midwest are all collapsed into a few brushstrokes: "ant lions," working together (as will the migrants), "started small avalanches." Weeds "fray." Earth pales. The wind, at first gentle, "raced faster." Humans, "huddled in their houses," enter this landscape only at the end of the first chapter, as if diminished by wind and drought and dust. Men endure the cataclysm by busying their hands with "sticks and little rocks." It's too big to take in. The first chapter is a dust poem about parched land, human impact, and human despair.

Consider the word "bayonet," a sharp noun that slices into the opening paragraph of *The Grapes of Wrath*. Steinbeck begins this book in the natural world, posi-tioning humans in the landscapes that define them. That marvelous, sonorous paragraph is replete with contrasts that set up the book's contrapuntal structure, chapter and interchapter: dust and rain, red land and gray land, earth and sky. The eye moves from sun to weeds, from large to small, and is caught fleetingly, I believe, by the "line of brown spread along the edge of each green bayonet." No other word in the paragraph is as strong. This militant word contains some of the book's aggression and anger; characters keep wanting to take up arms against the elusive oppressor: Tom growls at the truck driver, snaps at the gas station owner and the one-eyed man in the junkyard—"Cover it up . . . goddamn it"—glows angrily at the camp proprietor who calls him a bum and is "jus' stewin' all the time" in the first Hooverville. Even resolute Ma wonders what would happen if "we was all mad the same way." The word "bayonet" resonates with the militant title, a line from "The Battle Hymn of the Republic": "His terrible swift sword" is the wrath of God, demanding justice.

The bayonet of green shrivels just as migrants' lives shrivel in the Dust Bowl. And the "line of brown along the edge of each green bayonet" is the color of dry blood.

This is a book about what happens when growing things, green bayonets, turn brown and create an ecological disaster, the Dust Bowl—arguably the worst environmental catastrophe in U.S. history. It's a book in which water matters—even in suggestive details. Either there isn't enough of it or there is too much—torrents of water at the conclusion of the novel, bringing more human misery, a biblical flood. As Steinbeck knew, water was the ur-story of the west: not enough water resulted in the Dust Bowl across the Southwest; diverting it from California's Owens and Hetch Hetchy valleys created the Los Angeles and San Francisco booms. Tom Joad says he's read *The Winning of Barbara Worth*, a story about unscrupulous control of water rights in the Imperial Valley, a book that tested Tom's faith, given the ways that humans' unchecked greed despoils place. "I feel very strongly about water," Steinbeck wrote to Harry Guggenheim, publisher of *Newsday*, in 1966. "In Salinas we lived by a cycle of weather. I think it was one of 17 years. Then we had five to seven years of dryness. The earth died and the earth burned up and we became very poor. So, you see I am emotionally grounded in this theme."

Few will read *The Grapes of Wrath* to find out more about water rights in the American west. But it's a very good text to remind us what a land of little rain looks like, scoured by humans and then parched by nature. It's a lethal mix, as is the deluge for the unprotected, homeless Joads at the novel's conclusion. Rain nourishes, of course, but when you have no home because corporate agribusiness provides inadequate and temporary housing, then rain destroys—another kind of ecological disaster caused by human intervention.

In 2002, during the centennial year of Steinbeck's birth, Peter Matthiessen wrote that he was struck by the "deceptive simplicity" of Steinbeck's prose. The opening chapter of *The Grapes of Wrath* is the fictive equivalent of "all of it matters"—weeds and plows and dust storms, the microcosm and the macrocosm. In 2013, violent weather tore apart Oklahoma homes, leaving in the tornado's path haunting, broken possessions. Details crystallize a catastrophe that is beyond human comprehension.

Like his great modernist contemporary Ernest Hemingway, Steinbeck wanted to strip the English language of inessentials, florid adjectives and adverbs, literary clutter. Steadily throughout the 1930s, as his writing became more spare, he avoided reading Hemingway, in fact, because he felt the influence of the slightly older writer might unduly influence his own. ("I never read anything when I am working, no fiction I mean because it distracts me," Steinbeck admitted to his agent.)

Unlike Hemingway, however, Steinbeck's salty dialogue never seems studied—although some find it hokey. I don't. It seems to me pitch-perfect, concrete and exact, capturing the migrants' metaphoric speech patterns. Steinbeck's characters speak with the grittiness he heard from California workers and Oklahoma migrants—hearty sentences with raw phrases. The manuscript's rough language brought his literary agent, Elizabeth Otis, west in late December 1938. Her errand: to convince Steinbeck to omit several "shits," one "horseshit," and two "fucks" from the typescript of *The Grapes of Wrath*. Steinbeck reluctantly agreed. But he drew the line at "shitheels" in chapter 15. And in late January 1939, after John and Carol had read a second batch of proofs, he wrote a letter of mild complaint to his editor at Viking Press:

> The proofreader doesn't understand that I write dialogue by ear and that the form of a word changes according to its relation to other words. For instance:
>
> There's nothin' to do.
>
> There aint nothing I wouldn't do.
>
> In the second the g is there as in French because it elides with the open I. There are many such things in this ms and I can see how a proofreader

would go nuts. But I'm writing the speech as I
know it with my ear.

He wanted words and speech patterns to be the migrants'
own: "Those Okies were true language builders," he
wrote years later, "wonderful and incorrigible. . . . A people who can refer to dying as 'reachin' for the shovel
shelf' is capable of anything." As historian Michael Kazin notes, "From novels like *The Grapes of Wrath* to TV
dramas like *The Wire*, the blast effects of . . . streetwise
prose are with us still."

Back to the yellow shoes. The novel opens with Tom
Joad's release from the Oklahoma State Penitentiary in
McAlester, where, beginning in 1935, prisoners were put
to work in the facility's shoe manufacturing plant and
tailor shop. Paroled from prison, Tom has calloused
hands that testify to hard labor. He drove a truck at
McAlester, he admits, and spent a year in the mechanics
shop. And he might have helped make his new suit and
"new yellow shoes, and the yellowness was disappearing
under gray dust." Those "new shoes" are the first thing
noticed by the truck driver who picks up Tom. In chapter
3, the turtle's "yellow-nailed feet" thresh through grass,
and in the final sentence of that chapter the "yellow toe
nails slipped a fraction in the dust." Two species drag
their feet through the red dust, ecologically bonded by
drought. Yellow isn't a symbol of anything, but it is a
brushstroke in a drab landscape—dust covering everything. Yellow is bright, arresting, linking chapters and
interchapters, as Steinbeck does so insistently throughout
this book. Color suggests to readers: Look here—it might

be important. When Tom returns to his family, Pa notices Tom's yellow shoes: "Them's a nice-lookin' pair a shoes they give ya." And Tom agrees: "Purty for nice, but they ain't no shoes to go walkin' aroun' in on a hot day." Tom's impractical shoes won't take him the whole way through this novel—indeed, Al appears at the Weedpatch dance in yellow shoes. And Tom will have to walk in another man's shoes before he's through.

"I ruther jus'—lay one foot down in front a the other," Tom tells Casy in chapter 16, repeating the comment to Al, and keeping himself a little walled off much of the time. Initially, Tom's nice shoes march solo. Going it alone doesn't suffice in this book, however.

And that cryptic sign in chapter 15? It bothered a contemporary reader so much that he wrote to Steinbeck's editor, Pat Covici, to ask if he "would be good enough to relieve my puzzlement by deciphering one of the 'signs on cards, picked out with shining mica'" hanging on the wall of Al and Suzy's hamburger stand. "IITYWYBAD?" was a common enough sign in 1930s bars and cafés, perhaps leaning against a mirror or propped against a stack of glasses. What does that mean? a naïve patron might ask. If I tell you will you buy a drink? the bartender would growl in response. IITYWYBAD?

And the feeny bush? Steinbeck himself playfully answered that one, writing to his friend book reviewer Joseph Henry Jackson:

Now a feeney [*sic*] bush is about four feet high and has a brittle taste. Pharmacopeia lists its medicinal qualities as purgative when made into a tea and diurhetic [*sic*] when made into a mush. Mashed it grows hair, dried and laid in bureau drawers it is an ornament as well as a sachet. Its leaf is grayish green and early in April it bears [*sic*] a pale golden flower which is said to be used as a charm for attracting women and for causing bees to swarm. The feeney bush as you see is a useful, a traditional and a beautiful plant. . . . Why do people get so outraged at my feeney bush? Carol blusters about it all the time. You'd think she had been personally insulted by my feeney bush.

His feeny bush may be a private joke or Okie vernacular, but its presence suggests what Steinbeck meant when he said he created a "wall of background" for each story he wrote. Historical references, both social and natural, are resonant, suggesting layers of meaning and appropriateness. Both Pa and Uncle John jump this feeny bush, each trying to prove he is more aggressive. That's the patriarchal model they come from: competitive, hierarchical.

Why does this novel begin in Oklahoma, with the bulldozed home, the gathered family, the cackling used-car salesmen, the ornery Hudson Super Six, the ribbon of highway, Route 66? The physicality of the migrants' world tells its own story, starting with dust, as if Steinbeck is working from the ground up, creating lives lived out of the dust that darkens yellow shoes.

What Steinbeck saw as Book I, chapters 1–11 of *Grapes*, is heavy with the sadness of leave-taking and heavy with details of ordinary lives: houses, furniture, windows, and doors are thrown into relief in this book because that's all that's left in a scraped landscape. Sometimes details are piled in lists or Whitmanesque catalogues: things to buy, "Used Cars, Good Used Cars . . . Checked cars, guaranteed cars"; things to sell, "Harness, cars, seeders, little bundles of hoes"; "doomed things" to leave behind; necessary things to pack, "the overalls, the thick-soled shoes," and, in the kitchen, "the big fry pan an' the big stew kettle, the coffee pot." The accumulated details of migrants' humble lives seem almost like the particles of dust that cover the landscape. The physicality of Oklahoma is present in this book like the "cloud of dust" that roiled across the Southwest plains, covering everything, a "dusty willow tree" and Casy's canvas shoes. "The raw smell of hot dust was in the air." Each sense is assaulted by dust—and loss.

This wasteland, doomed Oklahoma, has been home to the migrants, and their leave-taking is made palpable by the things they can and can't carry.

"Must take time in the description, detail, detail, looks, clothes, gestures," Steinbeck wrote in his journal as he was introducing the Joads, and reminding himself to focus only on "the little picture while I'm working." And like a drumbeat, his wife Carol must have reminded him again and again to do the same. She was his editor and typist and much more, and he listened to her advice attentively; indeed, he could barely write when she was ill or absent. The migrant story of dispossession is rooted—historically and ideologically—in the grim realities of lives reshaped by Dust Bowl blight.

Book I pictures the ecological disaster as an intimate human disaster. A one-crop system and a multiyear drought withers a bayonet of green and forces Ma Joad to burn her letters.

See the marginalized. Note the context of lives other than one's own. Study nature. Observe the thing itself.

CHAPTER 4

ƒCIENTIƒT AND WRITER

◆ ◆ ◆

AFTER *THE GRAPEƒ of Wrath* was published in April
1939, Steinbeck spent months "busily fencing out the
forces and people who would take my life and work over
for their own ends." With bravado he declared that "the
novel, as we know it, is dead" and that a new form would
emerge from scientific inquiry. He sought a "new basic
picture" in science. Composing a long letter to his uncle
Joe Hamilton, he explained his shift from partisan to
marine biologist:

> The new work must jump to include other species
> beside the human. That is why my interest in bi-
> ology and ecology have become so sharpened. . . .
> The bio-ecological pattern, having at its concep-
> tion base and immeasurably lengthened time
> sequence, does not admit the emphasis of such

crises as human unemployment, except insofar as they vitally threaten the existence of the species.

While Steinbeck refocused in 1940, this basic biological picture is evident in *The Grapes of Wrath* as well as *Sea of Cortez*. Both works bear the imprint of Steinbeck's long friendship with marine biologist Edward F. Ricketts, an extraordinary man. It is impossible to appreciate fully what Steinbeck was up to in *The Grapes of Wrath* without knowing something about Ricketts and the biological and philosophical ideas that knit the two men together throughout the 1930s: "is" thinking, group behavior of marine invertebrates (and of humans), survivability of species, the effect of wave shock on animals, as well as Ricketts's notion of "breaking through" to metaphysical awareness. One of John's friends wrote to Ricketts in 1939, "John Steinbeck has got me all steamed about your philosophy as a biologist—if that's not a contradiction in terms." It wasn't a contradiction at all.

Ricketts the marine biologist was "good at the whole [ecological] picture," as he said of himself. He was also a polymath, a man curious about Gregorian chants, Bach's *The Art of the Fugue*, Chinese poetry, Jungian therapy, art, metaphysics, Walt Whitman's and Robinson Jeffers's verse, Ernest Hemingway, and Krishnamurti. He developed a unique perspective that he called non-teleological, or "is," thinking (consideration of what is, not what might be or ought to be; a broad examination of factors influencing any issue rather than pinpointing single causes). "A stickler for factual truth," Ricketts also loved Faust, "to me, a refutation of reason and of its possibilities," and *Finnegans Wake*, "the greatest book I've ever come in contact with."

Five years older than John, slight of build, and gauntly handsome, Ed Ricketts drew people to him like a magnet, John included. The two met in 1930 when John and his wife, Carol, moved into the Steinbeck family cottage in Pacific Grove, two blocks from Monterey Bay. Ed had lived on the Monterey Peninsula since 1923, when he came from Chicago to set up a marine laboratory, one of the first on the West Coast, selling specimens to colleges and high school laboratories.

Ed was a self-taught marine ecologist when the term was used infrequently, if at all, in mainstream scientific circles. "I just like animals," Ed mused about his career. "I like to look at them, collect them, study, coordinate ideas about them. As a result of little skill but much drive, I have done work of a pioneering and much needed sort." Indeed, the product of his long, though technically informal, study of the intertidal was a seminal text published in 1939 by Stanford University Press, *Between Pacific Tides*. Each chapter treats different intertidal environments—the exposed rocky coast or sandy beaches or wharf pilings—focusing on what species inhabit and how they interact in each locale. In an era when biologists were trained to group animals taxonomically according to established scientific classifications, Ricketts's vision of intertidal communities was arguably revolutionary. Still in print, his text was, and remains, a classic contribution to marine ecology, a handbook in holistic thinking, seeing assemblages of animals as integral parts of their environment.

Ricketts was also a diligent essayist, completing numerous papers on diverse subjects. One discusses the four "growth stages" of poetry, from naïve poets to "all vehicle mellow poets" who capture the "beyond quality" of Whitman and Jeffers. Another examines "three levels of teaching." He categorizes men of genius in another essay, and in others considers depletion of sardines in Monterey Bay and ecological diversity. Both novelist and scientist spent hours analyzing all these ideas, as well as the notion of communities in the intertidal (similar to human communities) and colonial animals (similar to human bonds). Cooperation, Ricketts insisted, was as central to environmental understanding as Darwin's notion of competition. Ricketts also wrote an essay on "wave shock," noting that on an exposed ocean shore animals like limpets and mussels and chitons had to cling more firmly to the rocks in order to survive. This led him to ideas about zonation in the intertidal, bands of animals occupying different zones. All of this seemed so much like the tenacity of battered humanity. Science and ecology and philosophy are thus woven into Steinbeck's thinking about humans' relations to one another, to other species, and to the physical places they occupy.

"The whole idea of inter-relation seems actually to be pretty much the key-note of modern holistic concepts," Ricketts notes, "wherein the whole consists of the animal or the community in its environment, the notion of relation being significant."

Interrelation is what *The Grapes of Wrath* is all about. Steinbeck shared Ricketts's holistic vision of interdependence. Ideas the two men discussed are everywhere in *The*

Grapes of Wrath. In *Sea of Cortez*, where, my scientist husband notes, the ecological concepts they discussed together are laid out "like oysters on the half shell, while in the *The Grapes of Wrath* they are hidden, covered by a plot in a rich Cioppino." The account of their 1940 expedition to the Gulf of California is the Rosetta stone for *The Grapes of Wrath*, he insists. On one level, *Sea of Cortez* is a travelogue about a six-week trip collecting marine invertebrates in the Gulf littoral. On other levels, it probes the intersections among humans, other species, place, history, and metaphysics. "It is advisable to look from the tide pool to the stars and then back to the tide pool again," Steinbeck urged in *Sea of Cortez*. In *The Grapes of Wrath*, it is advisable to look from the Joads' land and possessions to their dreams and fierce commitments and back again.

Both books, Steinbeck declared, contained layers—four in *Sea of Cortez* and five in *The Grapes of Wrath*.

The first layer is the physicality of things, the world closely observed. Just as intertidal collecting sites chart the *Sea of Cortez* journey, the camps along Route 66 mark the Joads' trek. Steinbeck had a "wonderful awareness," recalled one friend. "A very keen eye for things. He was very observant." Start with objects: insects and gophers and deserted houses and rusting jalopies. Details contain the life of a people in flight.

For Steinbeck, as for William Wordsworth and William Blake, a child's lucid vision captures those essentials. In *Sea of Cortez,* Steinbeck writes:

> We have not known a single great scientist who
> could not discourse freely and interestingly with

a child. Can it be that the haters of clarity have nothing to say, have observed nothing, have no clear picture of even their own fields? A dull man seems to be a dull man no matter what his field, and of course it is the right of a dull scientist to protect himself with feathers and robes, emblems and degrees, as do other dull men who are potentates and grand imperial rulers of lodges of dull men.

Understanding begins with clarity. Steinbeck scrawled reminders to himself: capture a "child's vision" because "adults haven't the clear fine judgment of children." That meant to write with precision and freshness. "The story is fine," he wrote before he outlined the life of Mexican revolutionary hero Emiliano Zapata in the late 1940s, "but I must simplify it to the point where a child can understand it. I must make everything crystal clear. Then there will be no chance of a misunderstanding at any time about it. . . ." He said something similar before he began writing *The Red Pony* (1937), *Of Mice and Men* (1937), and *East of Eden* (1952). Start with first principles. Ground the reader in the essentials, the particulars of life, the migrants' habitat. In *Walden*, Henry David Thoreau does the same. In *Leaves of Grass*, Walt Whitman does the same. Both authors are alluded to in *The Grapes of Wrath*.

Steinbeck's prose is lucid. Sentences cast objects into sharp relief, like Sally Lightfoot crabs with "brilliant cloisonné carapaces" who walk "on their tiptoes" across dark intertidal boulders.

CHAPTER 5

A Journal, the Turtle, and Interchapters

♦ ♦ ♦

As he was about to write the scene of Tom skinning the rabbit, Steinbeck noted in his journal the book's unfolding pattern: "It must be far and away the best thing I have ever attempted—slow but sure, piling detail on detail until a picture and an experience emerge. Until the whole throbbing thing emerges." Steinbeck's awareness of layers is there, from detail to a larger whole. Language rooted in the familiar and commonplace may soar to the mythic, and this was Steinbeck's challenge—to assemble the bits and pieces of the migrants' lives and then translate that immediacy into a web of associations and layers of meaning.

Take it slow. Be deliberate. Let the Joads' world sink in. "There can never be too much of background," Steinbeck insisted in his journal. The word "slow" appears again and again, like a drumbeat, in this journal that he kept as he composed *The Grapes of Wrath*, the ur-text to be read side by side with the published novel.

Steinbeck wrote several journals of different types throughout his life. Sometimes he integrated self-reflective paragraphs into the work itself, as if fiction and life were nearly seamless. (This was his practice when he composed his second novel, *To a God Unknown* [1933], as well as a series of short stories in 1933 and 1934 and *Of Mice and Men*.) Sometimes, if his own work wasn't going well, he would reread his work diaries and then would feel better because, he realized, "I have always had trouble with my work." Sometimes he wrote journal entries in separate volumes. And sometimes, as in 1949 and 1950, he kept both work diaries and private daybooks, one marked "Secret" on the cover, as if the trauma of his second divorce needed space unto itself. (If he kept more of these intensely personal daybooks, they have never been located; he may have destroyed them, since throughout the 1930s he erased biographical footprints and shunned publicity as much as possible.) Two of Steinbeck's compositional journals have been published: *Journal of a Novel: The "East of Eden" Letters* (1969) and *Working Days: The Journals of "The Grapes of Wrath"* (1989). He preserved these compositional footprints, even transcribing the *Grapes* journal from manuscript to typescript, so he knew their importance. The differences between the two journals reveal the writer's intentions for his two "big" novels—his epics—one confessional, one reportorial.

While the *East of Eden* journal is expansive and intimate, much like the novel itself, the *Grapes* journal is terse, rarely confessional, a map of his "actual working days and hours," the 100 days he gave himself to complete the "big book" that he had researched for nearly three years. The ticktock of entries seems like a metronome, reminders of progress and word count and pace, here and there a pat on the back for a day's work well done, sometimes admissions of self-doubt. The document is muscular and determined, the word "will" appearing again and again as he wills himself into his 2,000 words a day, about seven typed pages. Writing days were weekdays, Monday through Friday, May through October 1938. Weekends tended to be visiting or drinking days: "If I am to drink anything, Friday night is the best night for it." If a day was interrupted, he made it up, his eye on the self-imposed deadline. One weekend, John, Carol, and friends had a "mad dancing" night and he danced more furiously than he had in his whole life. Writing *Grapes*, John Steinbeck the writer was on overdrive, his personality subsumed by the book itself.

The two texts he wrote side by side in 1938, the journal and *Grapes,* mimic his compositional method: contraction in the journal, slow and steady expansion in the novel.

Midway through his 100 days, he wrote to his editor: "The new book is going well. Too fast. I'm having to hold it down. I don't want it to go so fast for fear the tempo will be fast and this is a plodding, crawling book. So I'm holding it down to approximately six pages a day. . . ."

I read this passage to my students and anticipate a groan. It comes. And then I suggest that they shift perspectives and consider what a slow tempo means and why, in the twenty-first century, Slow movements are slowly gaining momentum: Slow Food, Slow Parenting, Slow Growth. Manifestos encourage "regional food," "small enterprises," and fewer activities for children. Or consider yoga. People pay money to take yoga classes, I remind my students, money to breathe deeply, to feel each muscle, to concentrate and participate in the body's power. Deliberate reading is as cleansing as deliberate movement. To enter a yoga studio is to cross a boundary into a place of serenity. To open a long book is to relinquish speed. The Joads' car doesn't go very fast. On the way to California, the family stops frequently, to fix the Wilsons' car, to bury Grampa, to bathe in the Colorado River. To read *The Grapes of Wrath* at a steady pace is to fully participate in the family's great losses and their determined movement forward.

The turtle crawls into the book early on, reminding readers, with his parabolic presence, that this book is not a factual record, not the history of an era. It's a novel. Novels, not history books, include little parables that speak to timeless issues. The turtle has a profound and multivalent message.

And one part is to slow down. For about half of *The Grapes of Wrath* the Joads crawl to California in an "ornery" Hudson Super Six as they set out with thirteen packed together uncomfortably in the sawed-off car, now a truck—one hybrid of many in this book of transitional lives and homes. When he crosses the Oklahoma state line, Tom breaks his parole and becomes a fugitive. He and his family, the dispossessed, are frightened and stunned by loss along the route—of Grampa, Granma, and Noah, and later Connie, who skulks off after a skirmish in the Hooverville camp. Pa is unmoored from land and patriarchy. Uncle John is guilt ridden and burdensome—to himself and others. Strangers are often hostile. All this emotional intensity cannot be glossed over quickly. To participate in the actuality, a reader has to knuckle down with the agony of the Joads' odyssey.

The turtle, like the Joads, crawls on, determined, unstoppable. The turtle carries his home with him, like the Joads. He is at the mercy of machines that might crush him, like the Joads. But if the turtle represents the migrants, so too does the seed lodged in his leg represent the potential for new life. The slow reader recognizes the significance of both the turtle and the emblematic seed he sows.

"Yesterday turtle episode which satisfies me in a number of ways," Steinbeck wrote in his journal. And the next day, "Turtle sequence stands up." He liked what he'd written.

Carol Steinbeck said that "one of the things John always wanted to do was write a long narrative poem. However, probably certain lyrical passages in inner chapters of *Grapes* and *East of Eden* may have satisfied this ambition of his."

Steinbeck himself called the inner chapters "sort of biblical."

Interchapters are like rest stops on a highway. Pausing, the reader uses all senses—feeling, seeing, hearing, touching. The interchapters pull a reader off the main road and allow consideration of the long stretch, the big picture. They serve other purposes as well. In 1953, a student from Columbia University had the temerity to write Steinbeck and ask about the significance of the interchapters. Steinbeck obviously liked the letter from this young man, and he wrote a fulsome reply:

> You say the inner chapters were counterpoint and so they were—that they were pace changers and they were that too but the basic purpose was to hit the reader below the belt. With the rhythms and symbols of poetry one can get into a reader— open him up and while he is open introduce— things on an intellectual level which he would not or could not receive unless he were opened up.

Lyricism, imagery, dialogue, rugged little histories—the different styles and subjects of the interchapters open up a reader, slow down a reader.

Chapter 5, Steinbeck wrote in his journal, "must have a symphonic overtone. . . . Have to make the sound of the tractors and the dust of the tractors . . . the smell of them . . . this is the eviction sound and the tonal reason for the movement." Tractors are monsters because the goggled driver ignores the natural lay of the land in order to keep lines straight, rips through fences and gullies, churns up dust like the wind of chapter 1, making the land uninhabitable. The Joads' particular story is replicated again and again.

Chapters 1 and 5 are stitched together visually. In each, the displaced migrants are frozen in tableaus, the men squatting and figuring, the women watching, the children behind, with toes working in the sand. Enter spokesmen for the owners—in chapter 5—and then Joe Davis's boy, the guy we all recognize who is out for himself, blinders on to others' suffering. And yet he too is caught up in the economic crisis that blights lives. He too is a victim.

Owners. Banks. The cipher we actually get to talk to. That scene has played out ruthlessly as people lost homes and lives in the twenty-first century: Not my fault but someone else's, over there. Something big and vague. In the midst of the recent housing crisis, the filmmaker Michael Moore insisted that *The Grapes of Wrath* was the novel everyone needed to read. That crisis continues today.

Then the "fierce" staccato of chapter 7, the used-car chapter, where the migrants are exploited by fast-talking hucksters. Steinbeck hated sales and after writing the chapter dreamed of his father's store, which had failed when Steinbeck was a teenager, and he still remembered that he "used to eat pies at noon hour and was ashamed of selling things." The syncopated prose seems another movement in a symphony, and Steinbeck had that in mind too—fusing poetry and music. Chapter 9 is about selling possessions, another blast at the capitalist monster. And chapter 11 is about the vacant houses—the end of part I, the eviction—and a return to chapter 1 and the land itself: "The machine man, driving a dead tractor on land he does not know and love, understands only chemistry; and he is contemptuous of the land and of himself."

End of part I, leaving Oklahoma.

Steinbeck said that the model for the interchapters was John Dos Passos, whose *U.S.A.* trilogy folds together newsreel and biography and headlines—capturing the tempo and the voices of contemporary life. Steinbeck also captured multiple genres in his interchapters: history, montage, dialogue, poetry, journalism. But as a reviewer for the *Virginia Quarterly Review* noted in 1939, "Whereas Dos Passos' social books are built on hate for an economic system, *The Grapes of Wrath* is built on love for the people bound to that system. It is a significant difference."

Slow readers down with poetry. When the novel was first reviewed in the *New York Times*, the reviewer warned his readers that it was a "very long novel, and yet it reads as if it had been composed in a flash, ripped off the typewriter, and delivered to the public as an ultimatum. It is a long and thoughtful novel as one thinks about it. It is a short and vivid one as one feels it."

Feel it. The Joads' is a slow journey toward the dream that America holds out for its people: land and home and job. The Joads' expectations and the road's realities clash in slow-motion prose.

CHAPTER 6

PARTICIPATION

❖ ❖ ❖

FOR JOHN STEINBECK and Edward F. Ricketts, participation was a first principle, "the most deeply interesting thing in the world," said Ricketts. For both it meant full engagement, understanding, and clarity. "The catholic participation in truth and beauty can arise only if a person has his entire horizon clear," Ricketts wrote in one of his own private journals. Of course, every artist wants something similar, a rapt audience. But for scientist and writer the word "participate" was a mantra, living into experience.

Music helps get that concept across.

Bruce Springsteen's "The Ghost of Tom Joad" is all about participation, a good beginning for a lecture or a class or a reader. The title song in his 1995 album of the same name is about those with "no home no job no peace no rest." That line alone is a pretty good summary of *The Grapes of Wrath*. And Springsteen's song of the road aligns perfectly with Steinbeck's sense of participation, engaging an audience, having readers respond viscerally and powerfully to a story.

Springsteen's, like Steinbeck's, is participatory art. The "I" of the refrain is initially "searchin' for the ghost of Tom Joad," then "waitin' on the ghost of Tom Joad," and then, after Tom's famous speech to Ma is paraphrased at the song's conclusion, Joad is present, "with" the speaker. The lyrical arc of searching for, waiting for, and being with that apparition pulls the reader into the campfire light with the speaker and with Tom Joad because the song brings him to life—for the I of the verses and for the I listening to the shifting refrain. Thus, art engages. Art asks the auditor/reader to share a bone-gripping narrative of suffering humanity.

Here's what Springsteen said about that when he played an openhearted benefit concert for San Jose State University's Steinbeck Research Center in October 1996: The "values of [Steinbeck's] work are more real today than they ever were . . . [t]o increase understanding and patience and compassion, to get a chance to fight that isolation that seems to be part of the American character. In *The Grapes of Wrath*, Preacher Casy calls that isolation the wilderness. That's what it is. I think John Steinbeck's work was to reach in and pull you out of that wilderness, out into the world."

Over the years, Tom Joad's name and that speech have become shorthand for engagement. Both title song and Springsteen's album resuscitate a fictional character's sense of urgency—Tom taking leave of his mother, telling her that he won't disappear from this world where human suffering is ever present. More oxygen was added when Rage Against the Machine released its version of "The Ghost of Tom Joad"—more every time Henry Fonda speaks Tom's words in a clip from John Ford's 1940 film of the novel. Steinbeck himself borrowed Tom's speech from another ballad, "Joe Hill," a song about a labor organizer.

And Woody Guthrie borrowed Tom's words. It's hardly surprising that this rugged little man, hitchhiking around America in 1940, would gravitate to *The Grapes of Wrath*. When he was invited to participate in a "Grapes of Wrath Evening," a 1940 benefit concert for migrant farmworkers held in New York City, he wrote the seventeen-verse ballad "Tom Joad," which ends with "Wherever men are fightin' for their rights, . . . / That's where I'm a-gonna be." His Tom Joad is a union organizer. John Steinbeck wrote a little tribute to Woody in 1967: "[T]here is nothing sweet about Woody, and there is nothing sweet about the songs he sings. But there is something more important for those who will listen. There is the will of a people to endure and fight against oppression. I think we call this the American Spirit."

Tom Joad's ghostly presence, from book to film to Guthrie to Springsteen to Rage Against the Machine— and to readers—conveys the notion of participation, engaging deeply in what's before you. Without it there is no understanding of the American spirit or anything else.

When I was editing SJSU's *Steinbeck Newsletter* in the 1990s, all sorts of tidbits about the writer were sent to me, including this one from Arthur Krim, historian of Route 66, who recognized that Kris Kristofferson's 1980

"Here Comes That Rainbow Again" draws on the lunch-counter episode to suggest Steinbeck's power of connection. Arthur wrote Kris and Kris wrote this back:

> What I really like about Steinbeck's creation is the heart. And that scene in the lunchroom is a perfect expression of the tough kindness of which we humans are capable. It never fails to move an audience and I think it's a good direction to be moved.

Heart is the reason that people like Arthur contacted me: they loved Steinbeck, wanted to let me know about this and that. "Heart" is the word that recurs most frequently in commentary about this novel—Steinbeck's heart, readers' hearts. Participation depends on emotional engagement, moving an audience, what Ricketts called "inner coherences both of feeling and of thought content" which lead to "deep participation."

Music helps make that connection, suggested both through Steinbeck's rhythmic prose and through his several references to music bringing folks together: "And perhaps a man brought out his guitar to the front of his tent. And he sat on a box to play, and everyone in the camp moved slowly in toward him, drawn in toward him. . . . The man played and the people moved slowly in on him until the circle was closed and tight. . . ." A guitar is a "gracious thing" in this novel. Steinbeck bought a guitar as he began writing *Grapes*, picking out chords—badly, apparently—he and Carol sawing away together, she with her accordion, he with his two chords. Then again, in this novel even cacophony is powerful: the Jehovites' feral meeting at the Colorado River, with "howlers an' jumpers" and growlers and whiners, affects both Ma, who modulates her criticism of the sect, and Granma, who falls asleep as they chant. Music soothes and unites. When Sairy Wilson sang as a little girl and folks came to hear her, "why, me an' them was together mor'n you could ever know." It's like praying, she says, "singin' an' prayin', jus' the same thing." Music is participatory. It is a sacred bond.

"Songs are the statements of a people," Steinbeck wrote in his tribute to Woody Guthrie. *The Grapes of Wrath*, said Springsteen, is "a work that resonated through my whole life and was as important as all those voices on all those records. It had the same kind of power."

Steinbeck insisted that he had the "instincts of a minstrel rather than a scrivener." Music in this book is prose rhythms, characters' speech, the gracious guitar, the whirling, uniting dance at the government camp—as well as the structural underpinning of *Grapes*. "From the beginning," Steinbeck wrote to a friend in 1939, "I have tried to use the forms and mathematics of music rather than those of prose. . . . It accounts for the so-called 'different' technique of each one of my books."

I've never been entirely sure what he meant by that. Maybe something like this, another passage from *Grapes*: "Many men can chord a guitar, but perhaps this man was a picker. There you have something—the deep chords beating, beating, while the melody runs on the strings like little footsteps. Heavy hard fingers marching on the frets"—fingers with calluses, left-hand fingers that stretch "like a spider's legs to get the hard pads on the frets." That melodic dexterity sounds like a pattern for a book, chords like interchapters, melody like the Joads' footsteps west. A former colleague of mine, Elaine Apthorp, said she thought that *Grapes* was structured like a ballad, the interchapters the refrain.

CHAPTER 7

THIS "MIDDLEBROW" BOOK

❖ ❖ ❖

As a newly appointed director of San Jose State's Steinbeck Research Center, I organized a fiftieth anniversary conference, "*The Grapes of Wrath*, 1939–1989: An Interdisciplinary Forum." I wanted the gathering to be as big and unwieldy as the book. I wanted to pack the halls. And I wanted to shake things up with the keynote speaker, Leslie Fiedler, a great scholar and disturber. While I knew his reputation when I invited him, I didn't anticipate how thoroughly he would upset the audience on that rainy day in March. Steinbeck's characters were stock figures, stereotypes, sentimental, he asserted. And furthermore—this made a woman cry—*Gone with the Wind* was a more important novel of the 1930s because it "possesses in the highest degree archetypal resonance" and its characters are "true myths, as none of the characters of *The Grapes of Wrath*, alas, are." He insisted that *The Grapes of Wrath* was a "middlebrow" book.

Rereading his essay makes me chuckle, not because a woman cried when he read those words, of course, but because Fiedler so loved the limb he put himself out on—he jabbed at the "second rank academics whose 'subject' is Steinbeck," many sitting right before him. In more careful times, that kind of in-your-face jive has faded from academe. But as much as I admire the man, I think he was wrong in his conclusions about the characters in this "middlebrow" book—although that term might have pleased Steinbeck, since that's precisely what he was after.

Steinbeck did not write an elitist "highbrow" text. Nor was pulp fiction his intent, "lowbrow" in Fiedler's scheme. Steinbeck hankered for the readerly middle ground that would blend the folk traditions of the Okies—their speech patterns and songs and fierce anger, their zest and humor and the great kindness of Ma feeding stew to hungry camp children—with the historical, mythic, and factual. He wrote this book for mass culture. Like his previous work, the play/novelette *Of Mice and Men*, *Grapes* embraces hybridity. *Of Mice and Men* the novel, he asserted, would appeal to a literate reading audience, and the play (Steinbeck intended that the novel itself would serve as the script) would reach the more popular, theatrical audience (he wrote three of these play/novelettes in his career). Middlebrow is a perfect term for *Of Mice and Men* as well as *Grapes*.

The Grapes of Wrath is a cordial handshake. In 1939, many read about poor characters for the first time, others found their lives in a book. I've heard that again and again. Former Oildale (California) resident and writer

Gerald Haslam writes vividly about his determined attempt to read *Grapes*, a sequestered book that, he discovered at last, was about his Oildale neighbors, about his own life. And the hand is still extended. A friend in Denver recently taught a simplified *Grapes* to ESL students, and one young Chicana said to her at the end of a lesson: "Are these people white?" Yes, my friend responded. "I didn't think white people were poor," said the young woman. Middlebrow endures.

To my mind, the kindly Joads are hardly stereotypical. I mention Fiedler not to dishonor his spirited critical legacy but rather to turn over that particular rock and consider why Steinbeck edged close to Joad "types."

In Steinbeck's 1952 novel *East of Eden*, the Chinese servant, Lee, translates ancient Chinese poetry into English: "I found some of the old things as fresh and clear as this morning," Lee tells his friend Samuel Hamilton. "And I wondered why. And, of course, people are interested only in themselves. If a story is not about the hearer he will not listen. And I here make a rule—a great and lasting story is about everyone or it will not last. The strange and foreign is not interesting—only the deeply personal and familiar."

Steinbeck said the same thing another way in the late 1930s, insisting that a writer can't write "about the proletariat . . . whatever they are, unless you have lived with them and worked and lifted things and fought and drank with them. . . . All the terms are phony— proletarian—bourgeois . . . it's all just people. Write about people not classes."

The Joads are standard-bearers of the personal and

familiar. "Make the people live. Make them live," he wrote in his journal. "But my people must be more than people. They must be an over-essence of people." The Joads are every family, every dispossessed family, that is— every family in exile, every family huddling on transnational borders, every family torn from a home. (*Pilgrim's Progress* is mentioned in *Grapes*, its hero everyman journeying from "this world" to "the world that is to come." A page after that reference, Tom takes a "pilgrimage" to places he remembers on Uncle John's land.) They are so fully engaged with grim situations that confront them— basic human needs of housing, warmth, food, and work— that the Joads and crises (or Ricketts's "wave shock") are nearly one and the same.

The displaced Joads are literally and figuratively located between a past they slough off and the cusp of something new they can't quite grasp. (Steinbeck loved emergent stories: a film he produced in 1941, *The Forgotten Village*, begins: "This is the story of the boy Juan Diego and of his family and of his people, who live in the long moment when the past slips reluctantly into the future.") Tom Joad and his family as well as Jim Casy and the migrant people all live in that long moment too. What they thought of as their land is gone; religion can't sustain; strange laws and customs frighten them—Grampa's hasty burial or fifty-cents-a-night campgrounds or the snarling sound of "Okie." To varying degrees, each Joad is pinioned to the past. And with varying degrees of success, each shoulders on: Uncle John reluctantly, Ma stoically, Ruthie and Winfield thoughtlessly, selfishly, and eagerly, like the children that they are.

And yet, in this askew world, where turtles are spun like tiddlywinks, corn is uprooted by wind, Oklahoma houses are tilted by tractors, and families are splintered, the Joads maintain a center, a deep-seated dignity. Immediately after Grampa dies, Granma comes out of the tent standing tall: "She walked for her family and held her head straight for the family." That may seem sentimental to some readers, but heart-wrenching dignity is something to behold, in books and in life. In *The Grapes of Wrath*, the family unit is the measure of our humanity.

Celebrating the gritty and commonplace, the homespun and plainspoken has a long tradition in American experience. John Steinbeck honors the dignity of ordinary working people, bound together by blood ties, common courtesies, and deep traditions. When I was on a team that considered a central theme for the Steinbeck Centennial in 2002, we came up with "Troubadour of the common man." Add woman and it works.

Consider what Steinbeck meant by "my people." Of course the migrants are fictional characters, thus his. It may seem as if he's playing God to the migrant poor. But I think he felt a deep psychological bond with the migrants—real and imagined—because of his own experience as an outsider, feelings palpable to him when he grew up in Salinas, California. In a town of "haves," he and his family were "have-nots," at least when Steinbeck was an impressionable teenager. When he wrote *The Grapes of Wrath*, he empathized with migrant woe and, for the most part, those Southwestern migrants appreciated that empathy and his advocacy. After the publication in October 1936 of his newspaper articles about

Okies in California, a series called "The Harvest Gypsies," residents of the Arvin government camp (also called Weedpatch) wrote him that there are "people who don't know how farm workers live and never would know if it had not been for your trying to explain and show them." After the publication of *Grapes*, other migrants made him a stuffed dog, "Migrant John." And the migrant poet Wilma Elizabeth McDaniel—born in Oklahoma in 1918, migrating to California in 1936, and late in life known as the "Dust Bowl Poet Laureate"—was a "gangling girl madly in love with John Steinbeck and carrying lead pencils and lined paper as a torch for him."

When Steinbeck gave permission for the Simon J. Lubin Society to publish his "Harvest Gypsy" articles as a fund-raising pamphlet, to be sold for twenty-five cents, the pamphlet was called *Their Blood Is Strong*, a line from one of the pieces. At the time, the title celebrated migrant survivability; today, it seems to some that it privileges white, Protestant, Southwestern migrants in California to the exclusion of ethnic workers who also harvested California's fruits and vegetables. But for Steinbeck, blood was a signifier of integrity, of family. Nearly twenty years after he completed *Grapes*, he wrote to his older sister Beth about his own family, a unit as solid as the Joads:

And we were strong. Damn it, we were strong. Dad once said, and I used it in a book, that he had little to leave us but good and clean blood. And he did and we have it. How fortunate we have been . . . [and that would not be so] without clean blood. We have never had the almost uni-

versal tragedies of dishonesty, or cowardice, of
meanness, of drunkenness or vice or cruelty and
we have never brought shame to our parents.

The Joads bring no shame to their state or their country—
even Uncle John on a bender does so in private, after Ma
warns him not to spill his guilt onto others. Keep it in.
Make do. Stand tall—"us people will go on livin' when
all them [selfish and powerful and rich] people is gone."
The embattled family embodies what Americans like to
think of as the national spirit—our country's heartbeat
powered by ordinary people, coping, leaning on one another. That was Steinbeck's intent. And that's the way
many, many readers experience this book. Steinbeck empathized with an abused minority, their integrity intact.
Middlebrow.

Carol Steinbeck said later that her husband fell in
love with the Okies and that it was love, and not a burning social conscience, that propelled him through three
years of research and composition. He said as much in his
Grapes journal: "To love and admire the people who are
so much stronger and purer and braver than I am." When
he amplified that admiration for a 1939 radio program—
submitting his responses in writing because he could not
appear in person—it almost seems as if he describes the
Arthurian knights, and in a way, that's what he was doing, clarifying why the Joads were the "over-essence of
character." I respect them, he wrote:

Because they are brave, because although the
technique of their life is difficult and complicated,

they meet it with increasing strength, because
they are kind, humorous and wise, because their
speech has the metaphor and flavor and imagery
of poetry, because they can resist and fight back
and because I believe that out of these qualities
will grow a new system and a new life which will
be better than the one we have.

There is a line to be traced from John Steinbeck's feelings
about his own family and home to his love of the Arthurian Round Table, whose knightly exploits he emulated as
a child (Malory's *Le Morte d'Arthur* was his favorite child-
hood book) and to his respect for the fictional Joads in his
"middlebrow book." "My people" come out of Steinbeck's
research on the migrants, to be sure, and his ability to
weave fiction from life. But that phrase comes also from
the deepest place in his own heart.

CHAPTER 8

ISOLATOES AND
THE GREATER WHOLE

◆ ◆ ◆

TOM JOAD STEPS into this book as an outsider, a loner, a murderer (in self-defense), and a maverick. He has many forebearers in American literature and life: Natty Bumppo, who stalks into James Fennimore Cooper's Leatherstocking series as a bit of an outlaw himself; Huck Finn escaping from Widow Douglas's to float down the Mississippi; Ishmael, depressed, taking off for sea with Ahab. As D. H. Lawrence long ago noted in his survey of American texts, our heroes are (at least in the texts Lawrence surveyed) isolatoes. "The essential American soul is hard, isolate, stoic, and a killer. It has never yet melted."

A flesh and blood isolato shadows Tom as well. When she first sees her son, Ma worries he might be mad like Pretty Boy Floyd, a bank robber, murderer, and folk hero who lived in Sallisaw, Oklahoma, mentioned several times by Ma and Pa. (In manuscript, Steinbeck shifted the Joads' home from Shawnee, Oklahoma, to Sallisaw, perhaps to strengthen the Floyd connection and perhaps because the etymology of Sallisaw, like his hometown of Salinas, is salt. Another link.) Like Tom, Floyd served time in prison, in the overcrowded Missouri State Prison, a decade earlier, from 1925 to 1929. Floyd is a leitmotif in this novel, signifying what "they" create, an angry man "loose an' goin' wild."

Ma tells Tom one version of the Pretty Boy legend: "He done a little bad thing an' they hurt 'im, caught 'im an' hurt him so he was mad, an' the nex' bad thing he done was mad, an' they hurt 'im again. An' purty soon he was mean-mad." "They"—the police and prison guards and officials and citizen posses—"run him like a coyote" and turn him into a "walkin' chunk a mean-mad." Ma wants to know if Tom, like Floyd, has curdled. Tom says no, that he "kep' away from stuff like that,"—meaning, perhaps, the narcotics, anger (Floyd punched a guard), theft, and shady friends that doomed Floyd. Others in Oklahoma felt as Ma did about Floyd, a man victimized by authorities; at his funeral, attendance was estimated to range from 20,000 to 40,000 people.

Ma's "they" of the law elides into "they" who push over houses, when Tom responds to her. And she, in turn, evokes another "they." "Tommy, don't you go fightin' 'em alone. They'll hunt you down like a coyote," as "they" did Pretty Boy Floyd. Over the Joads hangs a monster—be it the law, the bank, or the tractor that demolishes share-cropper homes. In California that monster becomes owners and the Farmers' Association. And over Tom hangs the fate of Pretty Boy if he lashes out at "them" on his own. Pretty Boy's story is a parable of the fall.

An isolated man can't successfully fight back. That seems the message of Pretty Boy. But "[i]f we was all mad the same way . . . ," Ma suggests in her first conversation with Tom. With that line she quietly strikes the book's major key. Isolation cannot sustain life—that is Tom's story and the basis of the ecological web. We're in this together, dependent on cooperation among species. Like his literary forebearers—Natty Bumppo and Ishmael and Huck Finn—Tom Joad is the comrade of a good man, and that man saves him.

Layer two includes interactions between species, co-operation as well as aggression. Friendship and family situate the "I" in the more capacious, life-sustaining "we."

Initially, Tom chooses between the paths of two men, Jim Casy and Muley Graves, both of whom he encounters on the way from McAlester prison to his family home, the first leg of his pilgrimage. Casy looks ahead, a vision-ary man, a man "off a-askin' questions." Muley looks back. Compare how Steinbeck introduces each: Casy first appears singing a parody of a popular hit of the 1920s: "Yes, sir, that's my Saviour, / Je-sus is my Saviour, / Je-sus is my Saviour now." Like his song, Casy himself is a hy-brid, a thinking man stalled, a preacher with no church, a man who is shedding his sexual and professional iden-tity and seeking another, unknown, definition of man-hood.

Muley enters with "Who's that?," paraphrasing the opening line from *Hamlet*. Uncertainty underlies this novel as surely as it does *Hamlet*. Muley is the ghost in this story, the old graveyard ghost who might ensnare a son looking for answers. Muley's inappropriateness as a guide is contained in his opening lines, as he gets entangled in his own words. Tom asks repeatedly, "Where's my folks?" and Muley just can't get to the point, instead rambling on about the past. His name, of course, is his destiny—stubborn like a mule, he's headed to the grave because all of his talk is about a dying way of life, stories of the past, his refusal to move on.

Steinbeck liked the character he had created. Muley Graves is a "fine hater," he wrote in his journal. And not a survivor.

But Muley is more than a hater. Cockeyed as he is, angry as he is, ready to shoot, doomed to be hunted down like a coyote, he also articulates the ecological disaster of the Dust Bowl more forcefully than anyone else in the book. The doomed man speaks true. Muley is Shakespeare's wise fool: "I know this land ain't much good. Never was much good 'cept for grazin'. Neer should a broke her up. And now she's cottoned damn near to death." Muley voices the important fact that it wasn't just dust storms that drove families west, but also a collapsed economy and poor land use—forty acres worked by sharecroppers, croppers in the novel, all planting cotton.

And Muley is eloquent about the meaning of place, the emotional tug of sacred places: he has been "goin' aroun' the places where stuff happened," hallowed spots of sexuality, of death and birth. "Place where folks live is them folks. They ain't whole, out lonely on the road in a piled up car. They ain't alive no more." In his pilgrimage to remembered places marked by significant life events, Muley shows that "rootedness," in the words of French philosopher Simone Weil, "is perhaps the most important and least recognized need" of the human spirit.

Torn from the land, Oklahomans were sliced in half, Muley recognizes, their blood in the red soil, their bodies on the road. Muley Graves may be crazy, as Tom and Casy suspect; he is undoubtedly doomed, soon to be shot down in a field, Casy projects. But he's also prophetic about the land and those bound to it and those who leave it.

Muley's ramblings also inspire Casy and, like a flash, give him a calling: "Folks out lonely on the road, folks with no lan', no home to go to. They got to have some kind of home. Maybe——" And with that, his direction is set, goal undetermined. And with that, Casy's role in this novel as Tom's guide and mentor is also set, Casy teaches Tom the difference between isolation and commitment.

Jim Casy's hybridity and indeterminacy, that trailing "Maybe——," get lost in what seems most obvious about the preacher—that Casy (JC) is a Jesus figure. Probably more high school term papers have been written about Jim Casy than any other character in the novel—just a guess—because of his initials, because he goes into the wilderness to consider his faith (and compares himself to Jesus—not as a prophet but as a lone man), and because he leads the twelve Joads out of Oklahoma. He seems a prophet, he is sacrificed for his beliefs, and he forgives his enemies, "You fellas don' know what you're doin'." Steinbeck does this a lot, it seems to me—builds an archetype and deepens it with shadows, deconstructing the obvious and tantalizing the attentive reader to see more layers.

As many have recognized, Jim Casy is multivocal, and hybridity defines him best: he paraphrases Emerson, Thoreau, Whitman, Blake, Bunyan—and Jesus. Everyone in the book wants Casy to remain a preacher and they ask for his benediction repeatedly. Reluctantly Casy obliges, always reminding his fellow travelers, however, that he's not a preacher anymore. And his sexual urges have been checked—certainly he takes no migrant women into the bushes. Casy is looking for another kind of manhood, that identity undefined in the beginning of the book. (I just watched *From Dusk Till Dawn*, my husband insisting I would like a vintage vampire-action film. What I hooked into was how much the disillusioned ex-preacher was like Casy: both are on a road trip, both are the work's moral center, both are sacrificial fighters, and both seek a new definition of manhood. Perhaps Quentin Tarantino didn't intend that at all, but I see Steinbeck everywhere.)

Critic and friend Louis Owens, one of the best Steinbeck commentators, quotes from *Sea of Cortez* to explain Casy: "And it is a strange thing that most of the feelings we call religious, most of the mystical outcrying which is one of the most prized and used and desired reactions of our species, is really the understanding and the attempt to say that man is related to the whole thing, known and unknowable." Casy feels related to the whole thing, and he tries to explain to Tom, the isolato, what exactly it means to be a part of a greater whole, encompassing not only spiritual renewal, but also activism, human solidarity, and environmental justice. Commitment is what Casy means. Participation with striking workers in a cry for justice is what he means because "Two are better than one. . . . For if they fall, the one will lif' up his fellow." Pantheism is what he embodies—knowing that "he jus' got a little piece of a great big soul" (echoing Emerson). For Casy, the universe has meaning, even when the God of his faith seems remote. It's what Ricketts called "breaking through" to spiritual awareness.

CHAPTER 9

WRATH

◆ ◆ ◆

IN FEBRUARY 1938, before he began writing the final draft of *The Grapes of Wrath*, Steinbeck was in a "white rage" over migrant woe: "I went to Visalia and for two days talked to the heads of families and it made me angry and then when I sat down to write an article the anger came up again," he wrote to Fred Soule, regional information adviser of the Farm Security Administration in San Francisco. Steinbeck had talked to over fifty destitute families on this research trip.

That soggy California winter, when rain fell steadily on the Central Valley, Steinbeck witnessed suffering that seared him. People were starving. Although he stocked food in the truck he bought for research trips, formerly a bakery delivery truck, the supplies hardly alleviated much suffering. He demanded that others help, "forcing" the head of the Resettlement Administration, the "good man" Jonathan Garst, to hire an assistant for the exhausted Tom Collins, director of the Arvin government camp near Bakersfield, and to send lard to hungry migrants. Steinbeck "threatened him with publicity" if Garst refused to deliver oranges to the migrants.

Steinbeck's own contribution was the written word, and he wanted wide distribution for the "angry article" he wrote that February entitled "Starvation Under the Orange Trees." In that letter to Fred Soule, he asked that Soule submit the article to San Francisco's new Communist paper, the *People's World*, apparently not concerned that association with the paper would mark him as a radical. "Try to syndicate it as well," he told Soule; "it might not be a bad idea to try to make a few other people angry about it."

"It" was Safeway Stores fighting surplus commodity distribution, he said. "It" was taking a 10 percent profit on relief. "It" was always the powerful Associated Farmers and the power brokers of California. It was agribusiness. And, in broad brush, it was the state of California that allowed starvation in the orchards. "Starvation Under the Orange Trees" concludes with this indictment:

> If you buy a farm horse and only feed him when you work him, the horse will die. No one complains of the necessity of feeding the horse when he is not working. But we complain about feeding the men and women who work our lands. Is it possible that this state is so stupid, so vicious and so greedy that it cannot feed and clothe the men and women who help to make it the richest area in the world? Must the hunger

become anger and the anger fury before anything
will be done?

Rewritten, Steinbeck's wrath becomes chapter 25 in *The
Grapes of Wrath*, the most incendiary in the book.

That spring his agent suggested that he submit another article about migrants to "a national magazine."
Steinbeck refused. "I simply can't make money on these
people. . . . I want to put a tag of shame on the greedy
bastards who are responsible for this but I can do it best
through newspapers." He was also invited to participate
in a nonpartisan discussion of labor in Berkeley. Again he
refused in anger:

> Your card alarms me . . . I am afraid of that word
> non-partisan. . . . The Associated Farmers are
> non-partisan. In fact, the word non-partisan de-
> scribes one of two kinds of people: 1. Those who
> through lack of understanding or interest have
> not taken a side, and 2. Those who use the term
> to conceal a malevolent partisanship. I am com-
> pletely partisan. Every effort I can bring to bear is
> and has been the call of the common working
> people to the end that they may have what they
> raise, wear what they weave, use what they pro-
> duce and in every way and in completeness share
> in the works of their hands and heads.

In the spring of 1938, Steinbeck couldn't shake his anger. Although his editor, Pat Covici, came to California in
early April 1938 to remind Steinbeck—gently but firmly,

one supposes—that he was under contract to produce a book, Steinbeck nevertheless "abandoned the long novel for the moment," the book he called "The Oklahomans," to write quickly a few more vitriolic pages, a separate book called "L'Affaire Lettuceberg." The (eventually unpublished) "short satiric book with a lot of viciousness"— "L'Affaire Lettuceberg"—was a burlesque of strike-breaking tactics, he admitted to filmmaker Pare Lorentz. It focused on Salinas fat cats, the kind of people he held responsible for the migrant woe. The book "has a job to do," he wrote to Lorentz, "and I don't care if it isn't good literature. In fact I don't want it to be. It isn't written for literary people." Steinbeck was hurling lances at the opposition, hoping they stuck.

But the title was terrible, and the attack on "Lettuceberg"—clearly his hometown of Salinas—was unchecked and nasty. His wife, Carol, hated the manuscript. He imagined that his gracious father would call it a smart-aleck book. A few days after he finished the diatribe, he destroyed it.

All that unleashed anger was therapeutic, however. "L'Affaire Lettuceberg" sluiced the "viciousness" from his system, he admitted. "Washed clean," he was "able to get back to the other with enthusiasm and I think some force." "The Oklahomans" became *The Grapes of Wrath*, his fury channeled into the book's interchapters.

Unbridled anger makes for prickly books. Even when glazed with satire, invective rarely satisfies writer or audience, rarely changes hearts and minds. *The Grapes of Wrath*, on the other hand, the "long book" he returned to after those few choleric weeks in early 1938, was literary, careful in conception, and intended for thoughtful readers who might, in fact, be nudged to action and empathy—not bludgeoned. In *The Grapes of Wrath* Steinbeck measures out his wrath in teaspoons: Tom's anger at the truck driver; his anger at the self-pitying one-eyed man in the junkyard who hates his boss; his anger at the roadside camp proprietor who charges two bits a night (Tom taunts him: "I'm bolshevisky"). And his anger erupts in the Hooverville: "I ain't gonna take it. Goddamn it, I an' my folks ain't no sheep. I'll kick the hell outa somebody." Pretty Boy Floyd signifies what happens to an unleashed angry man.

Anger flares in gunfire, clubs to Casy's head that crunch bone.

But unleashed anger is not the central thrust of Steinbeck's story. Anger is not Tom's story nor Casy's nor is it Steinbeck's final response to a system that starves children. While the growing wrath of the people is justified, as Steinbeck acknowledges, Tom Joad finds another way.

Throughout most of the book, Tom subdues his sharp retorts by leaning on others: on Ma, on Casy, on lessons learned in prison, and finally on his awakened conscience. *The Grapes of Wrath* could be read as a lesson in containment: Tom learns to contain his wrath and channel it to something larger and better than himself. Although he kills Casy's murderer (which seems justified), his conscience is also awakened by that blow and he becomes a crusader for justice.

Maybe John Steinbeck tempered his own anger in the late 1930s. Certainly he exhausted himself writing *Grapes*, subdued his own fury. But a dozen years later, he sat down to write another big book, *East of Eden*, and he was giving some thought to anger; a nasty divorce had leveled him. There is anger in *East of Eden* as well, more psychological than social, as young Cal Trask wrestles with his demons. In 1958, Steinbeck had this to say about anger—something to think about when reading *The Grapes of Wrath* or *East of Eden*—or preparing to write about the world today: "I think any young man or any man who isn't angry at one time or another is a waste of time. No, no. Anger is a symbol of thought and evaluation and reaction; without it what have we got? I'm tired of non-angry people. I think anger is the healthiest thing in the world."

Anger that finds an outlet, not Pretty Boy's patterns of destruction. Without fuel, no fire burns—certainly not social activism.

Sometimes anger and outrage in *The Grapes of Wrath* may seem measured in buckets, not teaspoons, and thus a little unseemly. "Then again," said William Kennedy, reviewing *Grapes* for the *New York Times Book Review* in 1989, "how valuable, really, is the seemly?"

CHAPTER 10

WOMAN TO WOMAN

❖ ❖ ❖

HELEN HOSMER, DIRECTOR of California's Simon J. Lubin Society, a group devoted to migrant relief programs, said this about one migrant woman she interviewed in the mid-1930s: "The lady with the book of memories wanted me to realize what she had come from. She had a past. She had a tradition. She had a culture back of her." Sanora Babb's *Whose Names Are Unknown*, a novel featured in Ken Burns's epic Dust Bowl documentary, conveys some of that same domestic pride: over half of her novel is about Oklahoma dignity, women bonding in communities, supporting one another. Caroline Decker was another woman witness of the 1930s, a labor organizer of twenty-two when she was jailed for criminal syndicalism, accused of violating a California law that banned "advocating, teaching or aiding and abetting . . . unlawful methods of terrorism as a means of accomplishing a change in industrial ownership or control." Decker had helped organize a strike. *The Grapes of Wrath* is "a great book," she told me in 1989. Steinbeck had a real "sensitivity, a sensibility about conditions, emotions." She felt that he had done "quite a remarkable job capturing real live people living. It's hard to project yourself," she insisted. You "have to be sensitive to project yourself into the life of someone else, those lives so alien to my own. . . ."

Did Steinbeck project himself sensitively into the culture, the domestic routines, the lives and traditions of Okie women?

When Tom returns to his family at the beginning of the novel, he startles Ma in the kitchen, and she touches his arm, then his cheek to make sure it's really him: "And her joy was nearly like sorrow." After that quick, wordless moment, they speak to each other again and again from the heart. Ma's bond with her son is one of this book's wonders. Their intimacy and trust seem always so right and the bond so palpable—up through the moment she last touches his arm, hesitates at the brush line, and leaves him.

Ma and Rose of Sharon have a different connection, woman to nearly-woman. Pregnant Rose of Sharon is, in effect, the "anlage" of "the moving, questing people." She is a seed. While Ma cautions Tom, already a man, to control his anger, she urgently and consistently teaches Rose of Sharon—newly married, on the threshold of motherhood—to hold in her fears, keep desolation in check, and absorb grief. Ma nurtures her daughter to dignified maturity, a simple decency that endures.

Some critics (mostly male) take issue with Rose of Sharon, a whiner. Even Pa says she's "nimsy-mimsy." I've always felt that she had a right to be a little nimsy-mimsy.

She's pregnant, unhomed, stressed, hungry, and abandoned. That seems reason enough for self-indulgence. But I suspect that Steinbeck lets her whine so that Ma can pull her back in, literally—"Us folks takes a pride holdin' in," Ma says—and remind her of Joad values, just as Casy's actions and his thoughts (not preaching) give Tom other ethical codes to consider. Casy models socially engaged manhood, a response to patriarchal hierarchy of the landed migrants. Ma models localized values of family and heritage, of dignity and self-control and kindness. Steinbeck called this chivalry, and in *The Grapes of Wrath* it might be called domestic chivalry. The first description of Rose of Sharon notes that her smile was "self-sufficient." On the final page of the book, that smile has turned "mysterious," the last word in the novel, because Rose of Sharon has learned something more profound about life than tending to the self.

Each intimate moment between Ma and her daughter is a beacon.

At the first gas station, the Joads' dog is killed on the road and Rose of Sharon screams, feels the baby lurch in her stomach, and frets to Connie, her husband. "I hear ya yip," Ma says to Rose of Sharon, telling her not to worry that her scream hurt her baby. "Git yourself laced up, now. . . . 'F you go greasin' yourself an' feelin' sorry, an' tuckin' yourself in a swalla's nest, it might. Rise up now, an' he'p me get Granma comf'table."

Compose yourself, lend a hand, get to work. That's lesson one. Other colloquies range from thoughtful to stern.

Ma is also a daughter, and she is about to lose a

mother-in-law, Granma, who is "awful sick" on the road
to California. But death is a part of living, Ma in her grief
reminds Rose of Sharon, putting into a larger context as
well Connie and Rose of Sharon's sex in the truck while
Granma lies dead near them: "When you're young, Rosasharn, ever'thing that happens is a thing all by itself. It's
a lonely thing. I know, I 'member, Rosasharn. . . . You're
gonna have a baby, Rosasharn, and that's somepin to you
lonely and away. That's gonna hurt you, an' the hurt'll
be lonely hurt, and this here tent is alone in the worl',
Rosasharn. . . . They's a time of change, an' when that
comes, dyin' is a piece of all dyin', and bearin' is a piece
of all bearin', an' bearin' an' dyin' is two pieces of the
same thing. An' then things ain't lonely any more." Ma
concludes, having reached the limits of language: "I
wisht I could tell you so you'd know, but I can't." Rose of
Sharon must experience for herself the ways that death
and life intersect, a holistic sense of life as experienced—
as she will, of course. Again, Ma voices the book's major
chords—connection, faith, and pride.

When the Joads arrive at the Weedpatch government
camp in California, Ma wants her family to act respect-
ably. It was a common enough sentiment for migrant
families who were down and out. Mourning Connie's
abandonment, Rose mopes and Ma, working as always,
gives her daughter stern medicine: "Rosasharn . . . you git
upright. You jus' been mopin' enough. They's a ladies'
committee a-comin', and the fambly ain't goona be
frawny when they get here." Rose resists; "'Git," Ma says.
"They's times when how you feel got to be kep' to yourself." The tone of Steinbeck's own firm-minded mother

is in that speech. When John was about the same age as Rose of Sharon, he had terrible pneumonia and two ribs were removed to save him. After recovering, he still moped in bed, and Mrs. Steinbeck demanded he get up and quit feeling sorry for himself.

Each time she speaks to her daughter, Ma articulates the proud Okie culture and the values she brings with her. A woman who has lost her house and burned her letters—the physical objects that bound her to place—will not relinquish intangibles, her Okie beliefs and cultural identity.

Mrs. Sandry, a resident of the government camp, is the most vicious woman in the novel—rigid and sanctimonious. In a novel about inclusion, Mrs. Sandry is a mouthpiece for exclusion. Keep "outa sin," she tells Rose of Sharon. After Mrs. Sandry outlines the evils of close dancing, Rose sobs with fear at the woman's threat of hell and damnation, and once again, Ma reminds her daughter about the boundaries of emotion, about responsibility to her heritage: "Our folks ain't never did that. They took what come to 'em dry-eyed." Following that, in what I imagine is also Olive Steinbeck's voice, Ma says: "No. Jus' shut up an' git to work. You ain't big enough or mean enough to worry God much." That might be my favorite line in the whole book.

Alternately gentle and firm, Ma keeps Rose of Sharon trudging forward, initiating her into the pain of motherhood: "Very near let you have a baby without your ears was pierced. But you safe now."

"Does it mean somepin?"

"Why, 'course it does," said Ma. "'Course it does."

It means that Rose of Sharon, the neophyte, treads the hero's way. (Steinbeck knew Joseph Campbell in 1932 and the two discussed the hero's journey as Steinbeck was writing *To a God Unknown*.) She has left a place of safety—both Oklahoma and her marriage; has prepared for the trial (birth) along the road; is stricken by loss—her child born dead, a mummy; and circles back to her psychic home, her heritage. Offering her breast to a dying man "mean[s] somepin" significant—and mysterious. "I never heerd tell of no Joads or no Hazletts, neither, ever refusin' food an' shelter or a lift on the road to anybody that asked," Ma tells Casy and her family before they leave Oklahoma. By the end of the book, the Joads having suffered beyond endurance, there isn't even the need for Ma to ask Rose of Sharon to give of herself. A Joad offers what she has.

These womanly exchanges are effective and deeply affective.

Gender and sexual identity are important to this novel from the first chapter, which ends with standing women watching their silent men who "sat still—thinking—figuring." (The final interchapter ends with the same scene, women watching men to see if they will "break.") Men use their heads—figuring—women their hearts. Preparing to leave Oklahoma, there is a ritualistic last gathering of the patriarchal clan. But hierarchies and gender binaries break down even here. While the men's deliberate voices first assess finances, the truck's reliability, the number of people it can hold, Ma's voice brings the family meeting forward: we "will" take Casy along. When they leave Oklahoma, not only do the ornery Grampa and Granma die, but patriarchal manhood fades away—literally and figuratively—as well. At the Weedpatch camp, Ma runs the family meeting because the men are "scairt to talk" about no work. Ma sets the standard: "You ain't got the right to get discouraged." Ma is the titular head.

"Woman got all her life in her arms. Man got it all in his head," Ma says late in the book, articulating what is evident all along. She tells her two men, Pa and Uncle John, that the family will survive: "Man, he lives in jerks—baby born an' a man dies, an' that's a jerk—gets a farm an' loses his farm, an' that's a jerk. Woman, it's all one flow, like a stream, little eddies, little waterfalls, but the river, it goes right on. Woman looks at it like that. We ain't gonna die out."

That oft-quoted passage seems ever fresh, a truth we keep coming back to. Recently, Hanna Rosin has argued about the same thing in *The End of Men*. Confronted with social upheaval, women adapt more readily than men. In a changed environment, those at the bottom of the ladder become more energetic, are more flexible and adaptable. Exactly like Ma.

Furthermore, Ma's communal sensibilities might be a case study for what Edward O. Wilson considers in *The Social Conquest of Earth*. Like ants, he argues, humans are ur-social, "true" social animals because humans thrive in multigenerational communities, divide work tasks, and act altruistically. Ma is the head of this ur-social unit, the Joads negotiating their way amid and with other migrants on the road. She is the bulwark of associative living, always seen in context of another.

CHAPTER II

PICTURES

◆ ◆ ◆

IN OUR CULTURAL memories, America's Great Depression is frozen in black-and-white photographs and films of eroded lives, eroded lands. No era in our history is so visually palpable and sorrowful.

Dorothea Lange took the iconic photo of the Depression, *Migrant Mother*, a woman with furrowed brow, her two children turned from the camera—shy, defenseless, vulnerable. It's an intimate and a mythic pose, composed to evoke the Madonna and Child. The photo was first published in the *San Francisco News* as part of the paper's campaign to support sanitary government camps for migrant workers: "What Does the 'New Deal' Mean to This Mother and Her Children?" ran above the photo. In effect, the headline suggests, nothing. The message was clear: California needs the federal government migrant camps so that the New Deal will help workers like this mother. The camera told a story, and that story invited participation from the viewer: feel this woman's plight. "Documentary is a didactic art that aims to look hard but feel soft," notes William Howarth. Documentary art of the 1930s takes account of the people's lives, "to affect an audience's emotions with ocular proof, the arrangement of apparently unselected scenes." Lange's anguished mother, published over and over again throughout the 1930s, did its job well, blending heart and intent. That photograph, in effect, framed a central narrative of the 1930s—a family's agony.

About a month after publication of *The Grapes of Wrath*, Lange and her husband, agricultural economist Paul Taylor, came to John and Carol's Los Gatos ranch, bringing with them a book of photographs they wished to publish. All three had been covering the same ground in the 1930s, although apparently they had never met before that spring day in 1939. Steinbeck would have known Lange's work, however, and Lange his, since writer and photographer were placed side by side in the *San Francisco News* in early October 1936 when Steinbeck's first journalistic pieces on the migrants were published as a seven-part series, "The Harvest Gypsies." Both Steinbeck and Lange put a human face to migrant poverty, showing what it meant to be hungry, to stand in the rain by a dripping tent, to have a car break down on the side of the road. Prose and photos were in the service of better housing for migrants, winning converts by engaging hearts.

Steinbeck loved the book that Lange and Taylor brought for him to see, recommending that his editor, Pat Covici, take a look: "It follows very closely the *Grapes* although done independently." Pat wrote back right away, suggesting that if Viking published the volume, Steinbeck might "do the running comments for the book." That never happened. *An American Exodus: A Record of Human Erosion* was published by Reynal & Hitchcock in late 1939.

Throughout the two-plus years he worked on *The Grapes of Wrath*, Steinbeck considered other visual/written collaborations, and those, like the project with Lange, never happened either. In the fall of 1936 he thought about a play "laid in a squatter camp in Kern County. Instead of stage direction I'll furnish photographs," ocular proof that would enhance the wallop. That didn't get written. As he and Carol edited Tom Collins's reports for publication that fall, he wrote Collins that he wanted to include "photographs of people, of the place of the activities." That project fizzled. And in the winter of 1937–38, he traveled with photographer Horace Bristol for a few weeks, working on a collaborative text, Bristol claimed, or, as Steinbeck claimed, a photo essay. *Life* magazine rejected the photo project because it was too raw for a journal that wanted to go soft on woe.

Early in 1938, before he began writing *The Grapes of Wrath*, he sent Bristol's photos to documentary filmmaker Pare Lorentz (who created *The Plow That Broke the Plains* and *The River* for the Roosevelt administration), suggesting that Lorentz incorporate images of farm laborers into his next film project about industrial workers, titled *Ecce Homo*. Pictures were powerful propaganda tools, Steinbeck knew, and he wanted to use every weapon available: "Words and generalities don't mean anything anymore, but I hope with these pictures to pin a badge of shame on the greedy sons of bitches who are causing this condition and it is definitely caused, make no mistake about it," he wrote Lorentz.

Two months later he asked Lorentz to come to California so that Steinbeck could "talk the whole thing over with you. . . . I have a feeling that you and I could work together and I don't feel that way about anyone else." Lorentz's stunning techniques of alternating close-up and panoramic shots in the documentary film about soil erosion on the Great Plains, *The Plow That Broke the Plains* (1936), undoubtedly influenced *Grapes*.

In short, Steinbeck was fascinated with the intersection of the visual and written arts.

As a side note to all of this, Lorentz himself met Dorothea Lange when working on *The Plow That Broke the Plains*: Some of the captions on her photos made their way into Lorentz's narration for the film. "My intent," said Lorentz of his stark film, "was to have the pictures tell their story," a "record of land, or soil, rather than people."

All these interconnections are a reminder of the close links between and among photography, film, visual arts, and writing during the Depression. Fieldwork dug into the truth of experience, and the artist's vision created a pattern from the facts. That vision was subjective, of course, something Lange (whose photographs were accompanied by lengthy prose descriptions) and Steinbeck and Lorentz all understood about documentary expression. What Steinbeck writes in *Sea of Cortez* could be said of all the documentary artists of the 1930s: "We wanted to see everything our eyes would accommodate, to think what we could, and, out of our seeing and thinking, to build some kind of structure in modeled imitation of the observed reality. We knew that what we would see and record and construct would be warped, as all knowledge patterns are warped, first, by the collective pressure and stream of our time and race, second, by thrust of our individual personalities." The intersection of careful scrutiny and studious arrangement gives documentary expression of the 1930s its incredible power to inform and move an audience. Prose, photography, film, and the visual arts of the Depression are intertwined because the empathic warp of these interpreters was so very much in sync.

Beginning in 1933 with the Public Works of Art Project (PWAP), government programs for the first time provided direct support for artists. In the 1930s, many New Deal programs were created for artists, writers, playwrights, actors, filmmakers, and photographers, a legacy that is rich and enduring. President Roosevelt is reported to have said to his secretary of the treasury Henry Morgenthau Jr. that "[o]ne hundred years from now my administration will be known for its art, not for its relief," and that may be so. A community spirit was infused into the arts, creating intersections of artists and writers. Although Steinbeck was not directly involved in these government programs (his wife, Carol, however, worked on the Federal Writers Project's *American Guide Series*, contributing to the Monterey text for the California guide), his documentary impulse was intended for optimum impact that was artistic, visceral, and political.

In 1935, John and Carol drove to Mexico City, where he met Diego Rivera and saw the work of José Clemente Orozco (illustrator of *The Pearl*). The Mexican muralists were educating "the people" with public art about workers' roles in Mexico's history—and that impulse shaped American artists. Artist George Biddle, a schoolmate and friend of Franklin Delano Roosevelt, wrote the president in 1933 about the social impact of Mexican muralists:

> The Mexican artists have produced the greatest national school of mural painting since the Renaissance. Diego Rivera tells me that it was only possible because [President] Obregon allowed Mexican artists to work at plumber's wages in order to express on the wall of government buildings the social ideals of the Mexican Revolution. The younger artists of America are conscious as they never have been of the social revolution that our country and civilization are going through; and they would be very eager to express these ideals in permanent art form if they were given the government's cooperation.

Perhaps Rivera was the first visual artist to stamp Steinbeck's revolutionary vision of the people. When he and Carol returned to the United States from Mexico City in late November 1935, Steinbeck was envisioning his next work, the play/novelette *Of Mice and Men*, published in 1937, first performed exactly as written by a labor theater group in San Francisco, the Theatre Union, on May 21, 1937, part of the Federal Theatre Project.

Art contributed to and shaped Steinbeck's political education.

And his prose is richly visual, of course. He wrote in pictures. A decade after the publication of *Grapes*, he described the process of writing that book as a "work dream. And that is a dream, almost an unconscious state, when one feels the story all over one's body and the details come flooding in like water and the story trudges by like many children. . . . My pictures have always been much faster than my ability to write with a pen."

The novel's pictures create complex visual patterns. Pictures are replicated, like the chorus of a ballad. The vignette that closes chapter 1—the standing women and squatting men "in the doorways of their houses" ("A real farmer will squat when he talks, sit down on his haunches," insisted Helen Hosmer)—is reassembled in the following chapters as Tom searches for and finds his old house and his departing family. Migrant tableaus are assembled next to the houses they are leaving. Owner men "drove into the dooryards" to talk to migrants. "Across the dooryard the tractor cut, and the hard, foot-beaten ground was seeded field, and the tractor cut through again. . . ." Machines destroy thresholds, collapse porches. Muley stands "forlornly in the dooryard" as the Joads turn onto the highway and cats mew on porches of abandoned houses. The book focuses on thresholds: "a front door hung open, inward" and "on windy nights the doors banged, and the ragged curtains fluttered in the broken windows." Steinbeck's pictures of migrant loss of home are framed by the openings they abandon.

Sturdy, gut-wrenching visual art reminds us of the

great inequities that doggedly stay with us. And considering all of this also opens up the limits and possibilities of images, of the subjectivity of truth, of documentary expression shaped to an artistic purpose. "The design of a book is the pattern of a reality controlled and shaped by the mind of the writer," is the opening sentence of *Sea of Cortez*. "This is completely understood about poetry and fiction, but it is too seldom realized about books of fact." We keep coming back to this little truth, and today accommodate the notion in what we call creative nonfiction. But to Steinbeck it was all one and the same—melding fact, fiction, and a searing visual record.

CHAPTER 12

"LOOSE AGGREGATIONS"

◆ ◆ ◆

EDWARD RICKETTS WROTE startling sentences: "Who would see a replica of man's social structure has only to examine the abundant and various life of the tide pools, where miniature communal societies wage dubious battle against equally potent societies in which the individual is paramount."

That observation underlies Ricketts's second approach to ecology, considering "loose aggregations of several species, or associations into which animals band themselves." Ricketts's professor at the University of Chicago, W. C. Allee, studied group behavior of animals, and this became Ricketts's own passion—as it was for a few other scientists in the first half of the twentieth century who called themselves ecologists and believed that the study of plant and animal societies would bring "biological understanding to problems confronting human society in what seemed to be an acutely troubled time." Conversations between Steinbeck and Ricketts went over these ideas again and again throughout the 1930s.

In 1933 Steinbeck was electrified by the notion of group behavior applied to humans—what he called the phalanx theory—and both *Tortilla Flat* and *In Dubious Battle* explore the ways that groups form and shift, ways that groups are constructive and destructive. When a human is part of a crowd or faction or aggregation, his or her personality melds with the group dynamic, and the group becomes a separate entity from the individuals who compose it. "The group unit is so strong," Steinbeck wrote excitedly to his college roommate that year, "that it can change the nature of its biologic units. . . . Sometimes a terrible natural stimulus will create a group unit over night. They are of all sizes, from the camp meeting where the units pool their souls to make one yearning cry, to the whole world who fought the war." He concludes that "in our group units we . . . are remarkably like those most perfect groups, the ants and bees."

Migrant singular is thus a very different entity from migrant plural. Here is Steinbeck's second layer. *The Grapes of Wrath* moves insistently from I to we, from Tom Joad to Ma and the family, to the Joads as part of the larger migrant saga, over half a million journeying to California in the 1930s. "Being more interested in distribution than in individuals," Steinbeck writes in *Sea of Cortez*, "we saw dominant species and changing sizes, groups which thrive and those which recede under varying conditions." That's pretty much what Steinbeck records in the interchapters of *Grapes* and dramatizes in the

Joad narrative: the power of groups to both soothe and destroy.

With the Wilsons, the Joads form a "unit." In the interchapters, migrant families, "which had been units of which the boundaries were a house at night, a farm by day, changed their boundaries" as they moved west and "at night they integrated with any group they found." The Joads' story is etched onto the migrant epic, the book rocking back and forth from specific chapters about the Joads to general chapters, or interchapters, about the broader migrant condition. Again and again in both the Joad chapters and the interchapters, this book shifts focus from a perplexed I to a shimmering we. In chapter 15, a waitress realigns her sensibilities to give a migrant father bread and his children two sticks of peppermint candy for a penny. And while this is a sentimental piece—the chapter was selected by *Reader's Digest* to reprint in 1940—its sweetness is made tart when Al the cook empties the café's slot machine, knowing it's about to pay off. He doesn't want either trucker or migrant to cash in. Individually, as Steinbeck shows again and again, migrants and workers are flawed, sometimes selfish, sometimes self-absorbed like Uncle John.

The Joads help the Wilsons. In the Hooverville camp, Al Joad helps Floyd Knowles fix his car. A family feeds Tom breakfast, and father and son, Timothy and Wilkie Wallace, help Tom get a job laying pipe. But however insistently this book demonstrates the power of cooperation—"twenty families" becoming "one family" and the "loss of home" becoming "one loss"—it also shows what happens when that migrant unit confronts forces that would divert, delay, discourage, and destroy them.

While Steinbeck etches the faces of migrants in readers' minds, he blurs the bodies of the opposition—power is sinister, nameless, faceless, dangerous, and hard to identify. The tractors that drive into the Oklahoma croppers' houses are driven by goggled men who are in the service of owners who are in the service of a monster, the bank. In the dark, occupants unseen, police cars shine lights at Muley and Tom and Casy. Sharkish used-car salesmen, heard only as disembodied voices, squeeze profits from jalopies and cheat the gullible migrants. When Tom leaves Oklahoma, breaking parole, the long arm of the law could yank him back to prison. "They's laws," says Pa when the family considers how to bury Grampa. And there are enforcers of the law. At the Colorado River, a cop with "boots and khaki pants and a khaki shirt with epaulets"—nearly like a Nazi—calls Ma a "goddamn Okie." And at the Hooverville camp, "[a] rusty touring car drove down into the camp and there were four men in it, men with brown hard faces." Before they arrive at the government camp, the road is blocked by men who wear trench helmets and some American Legion caps. Vaguely militaristic, always menacing, contractors and cops and deputies and vigilantes are armed, angry men with guns. In the book's most violent scene, Casy and Tom confront vigilantes in the dark.

Humans form destructive groups as well as constructive.

Once in California, the Joads encounter the biggest menace of all, the Farmers' Association, a thinly veiled

Associated Farmers, a virulent organization that oppressed the migrant workers with intimidation, low wages, citizen vigilantes, and twenty-inch pickax handles. The Associated Farmers was a well-organized and well-heeled group, formed in 1934 after a series of agricultural strikes in California. Throughout the 1930s, the Associated Farmers operated in forty-two California counties. Their purpose was, as Contra Costa County grower Philip Bancroft declared, to "smoke the Communists out," those professionals who "inject themselves" into an "otherwise happy and contented group," the farm laborers.

The other side had a slightly different spin on the organization: "Who Are the Associated Farmers?" read the banner of a 1938 publication of the Simon J. Lubin Society, a group dedicated to helping migrants. The Associated Farmers was composed of big farmers: "I mean BIG," insisted the Lubin pamphlet, farmers who controlled "more than half of California's agricultural output." These men had "other interests besides—from banking to canning fish in Alaska, to running the Emporium Department Store," and they owned railroads and steamships and banks and controlled Chambers of Commerce across the state. The California Chamber of Commerce was involved.

"The Bank of America is the largest farmer in California," Steinbeck noted wryly.

The Associated Farmers wanted to keep migrant labor cheap, accessible, temporary, and scattered—like serfs in Steinbeck's mind—and they cried "Red" when workers got together to resist intimidation. "The great owners, striking at the immediate thing," Steinbeck writes in chapter 14, "the widening government, the growing labor unity; striking at new taxes, at plans." The great owners feared that Southwestern migrants might be drawn to labor unions as were the Mexicans and Filipinos before them; a union is another kind of aggregation, a terrible threat to growers because unions demanded housing and higher wages. The Associated Farmers feared and hated migrants because they were white people bringing possessions and families to California, clearly intending to settle, clearly capable of organizing.

The novel threw down a gauntlet to this organization, "the great owners, who must lose their land in an upheaval." Revolution simmers just below the surface of this novel about searing injustice.

At various points in *The Grapes of Wrath*, migrants are compared to coyotes, jackrabbits, ants. Steinbeck's many human/animal metaphors don't demean the human species. Humans act just like other species—banding together for protection and solace, acting aggressively when threatened, and acting cooperatively when it really matters.

CHAPTER 13

The Salinas Lettuce Strike, 1936

❖ ❖ ❖

When I was working on another book about Steinbeck in California, I worried that the historical balance needed correcting, that I had written about one group, migrant workers, but not another, shipper/growers. So I interviewed a grower in the Salinas Valley. He wouldn't talk about César Chávez. He wouldn't talk about strikes at all. But he admitted that growers had been wrong to insist up until the early 1970s that laborers use a short-handled hoe, "stoops" bending over rows of lettuce and strawberries. ("A man . . . must crawl like a bug between the rows of lettuce," Steinbeck writes, "go on his knees like a penitent across a cauliflower patch.") According to 1973 court documents, "Some workers testified that the short hoe really wasn't much faster, but that the field bosses favored them as a means of knowing at a glance if the crew was working" (the assumption being that an upright person might be resting whereas a bent-over person was working). We were wrong about the short-handled hoe, he admitted. And he also admitted that housing for field-workers was a problem that Salinas Valley growers had never adequately addressed. Even today, many migrant workers who seasonally pick lettuce and strawberries in Monterey County, where housing is expensive, spend the off-season in Yuma, Arizona, where the lettuce industry relocates in the winter and where everything is far less expensive. He ended the interview with this thought: the history of the growers, shippers, and workers in the Salinas Valley has never been written. "Growers have their snapshot, unions their snapshot, but the real story has never been told." In part that is true because it's still being lived. In part it's true because the network of power is intricate and, today, global. And in part it's true because the state's history of the powerful and the powerless is wrenching and violent and shameful.

"She's nice country. But she was stole a long time ago," a man tells Pa and Tom and Uncle John as they bathe in the Colorado River. In the 1930s, and today, most California farming is corporate farming, muscular and ever expanding, as dependent on migrant labor today as it has been for over a century.

The "shipper-growers of California," said Carey McWilliams, author of *Factories in the Field* (1939), a sociological study of migrant labor that came out shortly after Steinbeck's novel, "the men who own, control, and direct the state's fantastically rich produce industry, are a strange breed, one that must be studied at close range over a period of years to be fully appreciated. It is a breed long addicted to violence . . . in the area of labor relations they are spoiled, stupid, and arrogant."

Steinbeck had a story about a grower he met in the late 1930s, John saying to him: "You keep calling them communists. What do you mean?"

"I mean any son-of-a-bitch who wants 30 cents an hour when I'm willing to pay him two bits." John called this "Salinas thinking," and it became "sort of a joke."

But in the 1930 Salinas thinking wasn't a joke at all.

In the fall of 1936, as the idea for *The Grapes of Wrath* first germinated in Steinbeck's imagination, he witnessed labor unrest in his hometown—and that violent episode left its imprint on the narrative he subsequently wrote. Salinas was the site of a showdown between grower-shippers—with backing from agriculture and business interests around the state—and the determined lettuce packers union. The Associated Farmers and a newly formed Citizens Association of the Salinas Valley wanted to squelch the lettuce packers and any future strikes, and to keep the Salinas Valley, in their words, on an "even keel. . . . We haven't any sympathy . . . with the fellow who rocks the boat." The boat rockers were mostly white lettuce packers, working in cold, wet, icy warehouses. (Fieldwork was handled "almost entirely by Filipinos and Mexicans; white men refused to take the back-breaking, 'stoop labor' field jobs," noted a progrower article in 1936.) The packers had requested exclusive representation for the Fruit and Vegetable Workers Union. Growers refused, calling it "preferential hiring" that would result in a closed shop. For two weeks in early September, tensions mounted, with the "sons of the soil," as the probusiness article called the shipper/growers, refusing terms offered by union organizers—"something new under the sun." Anticipating the strike, shippers had imported scab labor and consolidated behind one packing operation in Salinas, another in Watsonville, building ten-foot-high chain fences topped with wire around each "besieged lettuce plant" (as the *California Magazine of the Pacific Business* described it), and guarding each with "a squad armed with tear gas, clubs and firearms," as the other side noted.

A national spotlight beamed on Salinas's labor problems; the "Battle of Salinas" was declared in headlines after a September 16 confrontation. Newspapers throughout the United States reported that the lettuce strike pitted white workers, "the red menace," against "embattled farmers." In reality those "farmers" were organized into agricultural cooperatives with ties to regional trade associations such as the powerful Grower-Shipper Vegetable Association of Central California (formed in 1930) and the Western Growers Protective Association (formed in 1926 by western growers in the United States and Mexico), backed by a well-financed cooperative effort. And the "farmers" had support from the Associated Farmers and the Citizens Association, as well as railroads, public utilities, oil companies, ice and paper companies, and the California Highway Patrol. The network of power was vast. For the grower-shippers around the state, Salinas was to be the "testing ground for a new technique of strikebreaking—the complete mobilization of rural and small town public opinion behind the grower-shippers' labor program."

Years later, Steinbeck wrote about the more ludicrous aspects of this showdown in his hometown: a self-styled "coordinator" moved into downtown Salinas—Steinbeck dubbed him "the general"—who urged the Citizens Association to take up arms, fomenting that this was war: "For a full fortnight the 'constituted authorities' of Salinas have been but the helpless pawns of sinister fascist forces which have operated from a barricaded hotel floor in the center of town," reported the *San Francisco Chronicle*. That "general" directing a town militia seems the stuff of comedy, a satiric parody—if reality hadn't been so deadly serious. "Now what happened would not be believable," Steinbeck writes in "Always Something to Do in Salinas," "if it were not verified by the Salinas papers of the time. . . ." The general claimed that San Francisco longshoremen, themselves on strike earlier, were marching toward Salinas, their route marked by red flags (understood to be Communist banners) on the road to town—later found to be survey flags put out by the highway department.

In 1936, however, Steinbeck was in no mood to see the situation as ludicrous: "There are riots in Salinas and killings in the streets of that dear little town where I was born," Steinbeck told a friend at the time. "I shouldn't wonder if the thing had begun. I don't mean any general revolt but an active beginning aimed toward it, the smoldering." In Salinas was the anlage of change, of worker resistance to the abuses of power. The Battle of Salinas shadowed the gestation and composition of *The Grapes of Wrath*.

Rereading Helen Lamb's 1942 dissertation on the Salinas Lettuce Strike, I realized as I had not before how many of the names were familiar. Businessmen involved in the Citizens Association and the newly revitalized Salinas wing of the Associated Farmers had been Masonic brothers of Steinbeck's father, and their wives were his mother's bridge partners. John had worked for Mr. Pioda, manager at the Spreckels Sugar plant (a man reluctant to join the Citizens Association). Although the Steinbeck family was not wealthy, not a part of the grower-shipper elite of Salinas, Mr. and Mrs. Steinbeck were civic-minded and committed members of Eastern Star and the Masons, the Wanderers Club and bridge groups, the civic groups that knit this small community together. Mr. Steinbeck had been the treasurer of Monterey County late in his career. What Steinbeck wrote in *The Grapes of Wrath* offended his hometown beyond measure, his name unmentionable in some circles up through the 1980s. He betrayed Salinas, the feeling went. They hated the side he took, and with equal fervor, he hated their position. In effect, Steinbeck attacked his own heritage, his parents' friends, and his former schoolmates. In some ways, *The Grapes of Wrath* was, for Steinbeck, an internecine war.

After he was awarded the Nobel Prize in 1962, Steinbeck said this:

The thing that arouses me to fury more than anything else is the imposition of force by a stronger on a weaker for reasons of self-interest or greed. That arouses me to a fury. It's the one unforgivable thing I can think of.

That fury burned nearly as fiercely in the 1960s as it had in the 1930s—as it might today, were Steinbeck among us.

In 2013, National Public Radio's *The California Report* aired a series on sexual harassment of women fieldworkers. "I couldn't say anything" about the supervisor's advances, said Maricruz Ladino, an undocumented farmworker in Salinas. And the supervisor raped her. These women, many undocumented, are afraid to speak up because they are afraid of being deported, afraid of losing jobs. Twenty-five years ago, Sandra Garcia founded Campesinas Unidas—the United Women Farmworkers of the San Joaquin Valley. "At that time there was no one to give us information, to tell us how to protect ourselves" from pesticides or sexual abuse. One federal agency, the Equal Employment Opportunity Commission, does just that, but "many of California's 800,000-plus farmworkers" don't know it exists, or that one chief area of concern is gender discrimination. A 2012 study by the University of California, Santa Cruz, concluded that sexual abuse affected four in ten workers.

The war between the powerful and the powerless is shape-shifting. The lettuce packers become the fieldworkers that César Chávez represented in the 1970s and those workers are still sickened by pesticides and harassed by supervisors, plagued by inadequate housing, and ensnared by immigration regulations and fences along the border.

CHAPTER 14

HISTORY ON THE OUTSIDE

◆ ◆ ◆

RICKETTS'S THIRD METHOD of ecological understanding is consideration of the complete life histories of relevant species. To note the Joads' relation to history is a large undertaking—Steinbeck's third layer of complexity. Contemporary, American, ancient, and mythic histories are wrapped around and threaded through this novel. "If only I could do this book properly it would be one of the really fine books and a truly American book," Steinbeck wrote.

The first edition asserted its American identity on the outside: dust jacket, stamped cover, endpapers. The publisher's intent, reinforced by Steinbeck's insistence on having Julia Ward Howe's "Battle Hymn of the Republic" printed on the endpapers, was to have no one say that *The Grapes of Wrath* was a Communist text.

The painting on the dust jacket, wrapping around the spine of the book, is a softly colored rendering of cars heading down the road toward blue mountains. In the foreground a jalopy is packed with belongings, a family, and a dog. A standing man in blue overalls, his back to the viewer, looks to the blue mountains; his wife and child, seated at either side, also gaze west. The road that curves to those mountains is lined with loaded cars, looking very much like a wagon train. A line cut of the painting is etched on the novel's buff cover (the color of dust) and was maintained in hardbound printings through the fortieth printing in 1978.

The artist was Elmer Hader, California native and a man whose work Steinbeck admired (he created the cover of *The Long Valley* as well—later, *East of Eden* and *The Winter of Our Discontent*). When Hader was hired for the job, Viking offered him a $75 commission and asked for preliminary sketches. On November 17, 1938, Viking sent Hader an abstract of the novel's plot, "a modern pioneering trek to the green valleys of California." Milton Glick, Viking's artistic director, instructed Hader to create "a panorama scene of the farmers moving westward, probably using every variety of modern conveyance instead of the covered wagon of earlier pioneer days." The cover "should not be one of dejection but of new hope." In December, Glick approved the final sketch, suggesting only that Hader add "additional feeling of dustiness in the air and dryness in the land."

Clearly, Glick wanted Hader's art to align with a westering tradition, of families journeying to Edenic California. Steinbeck's term for the national saga is from *The Red Pony*, where Jody Tiflin, a boy of nine, listens raptly to his grandfather's tales of the mythic west: "He

wished he could have been living in the heroic time. . . .
A race of giants had lived then, fearless men, men of a
staunchness unknown in this day. Jody thought of the
wide plains and of the wagons moving across like centi-
pedes. He thought of Grandfather on a huge white horse,
marshaling the people. Across his mind marched the
great phantoms, and they marched off the earth and they
were gone."

Hader's art links the Joads' saga to Jody's race of giants and the American myth of pioneer hardship, hope,
and expectation. In the national psyche, westering was a
drama of renewal, its end point a home and land and
subsistence. The majestic mountains in the background
promise an Edenic west that is as much the Joads' as it is
Jody's—as it is America's, a new beginning beyond the
cerulean peaks. Hader's landscape is visionary, not de-
picting any particular point along Route 66: "I seen it on
a map," Ma tells Tom, "big mountains like on a post
card, an' we're goin' right through 'em."

That dream propels the Joads. Visionary California
hangs over their journey, each character articulating a
personalized slice of Heaven, even as that chimera is un-
dercut nearly as soon as it is uttered. In chapter 10, Ma
contemplates domestic bliss: "How nice it's gonna be,
maybe, in California. Never cold. An' fruit ever'place, an'
people just bein' in the nicest places, little white houses
in among the orange trees." (Tom tells her that he met a
Californian who said that fruit pickers live in "dirty ol'
camps an' don't hardly get enough to eat.") Granpa is
going to "pick me a wash tub full a grapes, an' I'm gonna

set in 'em, an' scrooge aroun', an' let the juice run down my pants," a sensual fantasy if ever there was one. (And darkened in the next lines by the memory of his sneaky brother, a "son of a bitch, he was" who went west forty years earlier.) Casy follows with Whitmanesque expansiveness about the western migration, evoking the egalitarian spirit in Whitman's *Leaves of Grass*:

> I'm gonna work in the fiel's, in the green fiel's, an' I'm gonna be near to folks. I ain't gonna try to teach 'em nothin'. I'm gonna try to learn. Gonna learn why the folks walks in the grass, gonna hear 'em talk, gonna hear 'em sing. Gonna listen to kids eatin' mush. Gonna hear husban' an' wife a poundin' the mattress in the night. Gonna eat with 'em an' learn. . . . Gonna lay in the grass, open an' honest with anybody that'll have me. Gonna cuss an' swear an' hear the poetry of folks talkin'. All that's holy, all that's what I didn' understan'. All them things is the good things.

(And he then admits he's a lonely fella.) Possibilities voiced are shadowed, just as California, of course, proves no Eden for the Joads.

The cover art promises more than the book delivers. Hope sells books, of course, and hope keeps the Joads going. And hope for a better life is why the Joads, the salt of the earth, continue to signify an American spirit we don't want to relinquish. We fervently want to believe that Americans make it over the blue summit.

Steinbeck was far more concerned with the endpapers than the dust jacket (although he liked Hader's painting). He insisted that words and music of "The Battle Hymn of the Republic," source of the title, be printed on the endpapers. As Carol, John, and Elizabeth Otis wired to Covici, the song "disarms in advance any accusation of radicalism and will weld the American reader to the subject matter more completely." Both Carol and John wanted the anthem's rhythm to thrum in readers' minds; the song is a march and "this book is a kind of march," Steinbeck wrote his agent. Its stirring, patriotic call for freedom in "our own revolutionary tradition" segues into a book with the same moral fervor. The lines suggest evangelical and activist zeal, the triumph of righteous wrath:

> *Mine eyes have seen the glory of the coming of the*
> *   Lord;*
> *He is trampling out the vintage where the grapes of*
> *   wrath are stored;*
> *He hath loosed the fateful lightning of His terrible*
> *   swift sword;*
> *   His truth is marching on.*
> *I have seen Him in the watch-fires of a hundred*
> *   circling camps;*
> *They have builded Him an altar in the evening*
> *   dews and damps;*
> *I can read His righteous sentence by the dim and*
> *   flaring lamps;*
> *   His day is marching on.*

I have read a fiery gospel writ in burnished rows of
    steel;
"As ye deal with my contemners, so with you my
    grace shall deal;
Let the Hero, born of woman, crush the serpent
    with his heel,
       Since God is marching on."
He has sounded forth the trumpet that shall never
    call retreat;
He is sifting out the hearts of men before His
    judgment-seat;
Oh, be swift, my soul, to answer Him! Be jubilant,
    my feet!
       Our God is marching on.
In the beauty of the lilies Christ was born across
    the sea,
With a glory in his bosom that transfigures you
    and me,
As he died to make men holy, let us die to make
    men free,
       While God is marching on.

CHORUS

Glory, glory, hallelujah! Glory, glory, Hallelujah!
Glory, glory, hallelujah! His truth is marching on.

To include the lyrics is appropriate in many ways. The Joads' quest is biblical, an epic journey to the promised land. The book's title echoes the Revelation: "So the angel swung his sickle on the earth and gathered the vintage of the earth, and threw it into the great wine press of the wrath of God" (14:19). Like many Southwest migrants, the Joads were evangelicals, fierce believers, even if not churchgoers—an army of the righteous, marching on by the will of God.

And Howe's lyrics are patriotic, sung during the Civil War to the tune of "John Brown's body lies a mouldering in the grave, / His soul's marching on!" and thus linking the anthem to the abolitionist movement. By implication, then, the Joads' plight is associated with the slaves' struggle for freedom. Certainly Steinbeck saw the migrants as oppressed and abused: "I've seen such terrific things in the squatters' camps that I can't think out of them right now," he wrote to Elizabeth Otis after his first investigative trip. "There's Civil War making right under my nose. I've got to see it and feel it." By 1938, as he was beginning the final draft of *The Grapes of Wrath*, his "thesis," as he termed it, was that the migrants were treated as serfs and that California agriculture depended on serfs and "slaves" to pick crops (chapter 19).

It is not accidental, one supposes, that another great American protest novel, *Uncle Tom's Cabin*, shadows Steinbeck's epic. Both he and Harriet Beecher Stowe were crusaders for justice. Both were "moved by a great wave of pity" toward the powerless, notes Joseph Henry Jackson in his introduction to the 1940 Limited Editions Club edition of *Grapes*. *Uncle Tom's Cabin* is this novel's literary progenitor.

After Carol came up with the title in late August, midway through composition, Steinbeck wrote to Eric

Thomsen, among others, asking if he liked it. Thomsen's enthusiasm was expansive: the title called "directly to the accepted notions of common people about right and wrong." Thomsen continued his praise: "There is another reason for liking a title from something so venerable in our revolutionary past; it will not be so easy (as some have found it in the case of *In Dubious Battle*) to dismiss the book as communist propaganda. For it will be in the direct succession of our best historic right to civil disobedience in the face of intolerable wrong." That's a succinct statement about why Carol's title was so very, very good.

A few months later, Pat Covici sent Steinbeck a present, "a copy of the *Atlantic Monthly* . . . the issue that contains the first publication of 'The Battle Hymn of the Republic' and for this reason I thought you might enjoy owning it. Feb. 1862."

CHAPTER 15

"THEY'S A LOT A FELLAS WANTA KNOW WHAT REDS IS."

◆ ◆ ◆

JOHN STEINBECK WAS a lifelong Democrat, never a Communist, even though he edged close to the cause in the mid- to late 1930s. Layer three—life histories embedded in the novel—also includes the story of Communist labor organizers, who, during the 1930s, helped coordinate a series of furious strikes in California fields.

I once interviewed Caroline Decker, who helped organize the 1933 agricultural strikes in California, for which she was charged with criminal syndicalism and imprisoned for three years. But at the time, she told me, she wasn't even sure she was a member of the party, never having paid any dues. "If you said, 'Hey, I'm a Communist,' everyone believed you." Caroline Decker was a young woman willing to fight for labor rights at age nineteen, one of a "motley bunch of ignoramuses" who really "did not know" quite what they were doing, she said. The Communist organizers were certainly "not a highly organized or well-financed group. They were idealists, willing to plunge where angels fear to tread. . . . Babes in the woods," in her words. Perhaps not quite that, but from 1933 to 1939, the Communist Party's membership in America tripled, and the party attracted many liberals: in Decker's words, they were living at a time of "great need and felt very strongly about rights."

It was a "very dangerous" time to do what she did, organizing workers in the Pennsylvania coal mines at nineteen, in the fields of California at twenty and twenty-one. But, she added, "If you weren't attracted to communism in the 1930s you were a hunk of protoplasm." With the collapse of capitalism, with banks failing and farms going under and people living with no safety net and little food, an alternate system seemed preferable to capitalism.

In the mid-1930s, Steinbeck's Carmel neighbor Lincoln Steffens convinced John and Carol to attend meetings of the local John Reed Club, although neither joined the fiery little Communist group, about thirty strong in Carmel. They weren't "joiners," said the club's founder. "John was a careful, meticulous observer" and, claimed Steffens's wife, Ella Winter, "very shy." When Steffens suggested that Steinbeck write about labor conditions in California, the writer was intrigued. Steffens helped arrange meetings between Steinbeck and labor organizers who were hiding out in the Monterey region.

A couple of years earlier the Communist Party had sidled into California when the wages plummeted from

an average of 25–30 cents an hour in the 1920s to sometimes half that in the early 1930s. As worker dissatisfac-
tion simmered, labor organizers fueled their discontent.
In Decker's eyes, it was a boil ready to pop. In their efforts to organize California field-workers, the organizers
were pitted against mighty growers and shippers as well
as powerful business interests throughout the state. A
nasty strike had broken out in Central Valley orchards in
1933 at the Tagus Ranch near Tulare, operated by H. C.
Merritt Jr., who grew peaches—delicate and necessary to
pick quickly. In Visalia, two workers were gunned down
by growers during a peaceful demonstration. In Arvin, a
Mexican worker was killed. The growers blamed the labor unrest on the Communists: "For several years we
farmers have been on the firing line in the fight against
communism," Philip S. Bancroft, president of the Contra
Costa Associated Farmers, told a gathering at San Francisco's Commonwealth Club in 1935.

   In early 1934, Steinbeck intended to write a biography
of one of these labor organizers. But as he warmed to his
subject, as he heeded the advice of his agent to write fiction rather than nonfiction, and as labor unrest erupted
closer at hand—a San Francisco longshoremen's strike
during the summer of 1934 closed down shipping in
the city—his commitment to the workers deepened and
he wrote a novel instead, a searing and bleak strike novel
called *In Dubious Battle*, the title taken from a passage in
Milton's *Paradise Lost*. It's a book without a hero, certainly, but with several flawed representatives of each
group: workers, organizers, and owners. All are engaged
in a battle whose outcome is indeed dubious: the owners

are greedy and violent; the organizers turn ruthless and selfish; and the workers are fearful and victimized—and on occasion also selfish.

The novel, Steinbeck insisted, was as much psychological as social: "I wanted to get over unrest and irritation and slow sullen movement breaking out now and then in fierce eruptions. . . . There is a cycle in the life of a man but there is no ending in the life of Man. I tried to indicate this by stopping on a high point, leaving out any conclusion." It's a comment that says something about *The Grapes of Wrath* as well.

When Steffens died in 1936, Steinbeck contributed to a memorial edition of Steffens's *Pacific Weekly*—that gesture was later held against him, when the FBI investigated his activities of the late 1930s.

In 1937, he went to Moscow for some unrevealed purpose, probably having something to do with the party. And he wanted his angriest diatribe against growers, the 1938 essay titled "Starvation Under the Orange Trees," published in a Communist newspaper, San Francisco's *People's World*.

Like others, Steinbeck drew a curtain over his politics and activities in the late 1930s. Given the Communist Party's small size, a "quite remarkable" number of artists and writers were sympathetic to the party's vigorous call for rights and equity in the 1930s, as Michael Kazin notes in *American Dreamers: How the Left Changed a Nation*: "[a]rtists who, while not members, had spent many evenings in the party's milieu; created *Citizen Kane*, *Death of a Salesman*, 'Fanfare for the Common Man' [Aaron Copland also composed music for Steinbeck's films *Of*

Mice and Men (1940) and *The Red Pony* (1948)], *For Whom the Bell Tolls, Yertle the Turtle, Invisible Man*; and wrote the screenplay for *Casablanca* and the lyrics for *The Wizard of Oz*." Add to that *In Dubious Battle, Of Mice and Men*, and *The Grapes of Wrath*.

While Steinbeck was never blacklisted, he was investigated by the FBI after *The Grapes of Wrath* was published, his neighbors and friends questioned. Most of Steinbeck's friends avoided saying much: "Subject is very sensitive and sentimental; is deeply devoted to his friends," investigators noted after interviewing a Los Gatos buddy. When Pare Lorentz was appointed to the U.S. Air Transport Command to make pilot training films, he reported to headquarters in Washington and was asked to check in with army intelligence: "Do you know John Steinbeck?" Yes, said Pare. "Do you think he's a Communist?" Pare responded that they had never discussed the party. Other friends and neighbors in California, when similarly questioned, defended John's loyalty as well. But according to Lorentz, the head of the navy didn't want John to have a commission during World War II and so Steinbeck was barred from service. John blamed Carol for registering as a Communist in 1938. "She did it to annoy the Associated Farmers."

In the final chapter of *American Dreamers*, "Rebels Without a Movement, 1980s–2010," Kazin notes that communism "did teach a brutal, unforgettable lesson about the perils of utopianism as a governing faith." Steinbeck knew that when he created Mac and Jim, his ruthless idealist-organizers in *In Dubious Battle*. "But," Kazin continues, "the utopian impulse should not be smothered under a patchwork quilt of policy prescriptions. . . . Reformers from above always needed the pressure of left-wing movements from below—from the abolitionists, the Socialists, and the Popular Front to the advocates of black and Latino power, radical feminism, and environmental rescue."

Steinbeck's reformist zeal, while not overtly socialist or communist, seems to edge close to each. Tom Joad's final words to Ma are a sermonic call for grassroots collective engagement. But his is an egalitarian notion that reverberates throughout American politics and history and letters—not a communist but a democratic ideal. United we stand.

CHAPTER 16

History on the Inside

❖ ❖ ❖

WHAT STEINBECK CALLED the "wall of background" necessary to his fiction—*Grapes'* third layer—includes the haphazard history of Oklahoma land settlement. Grampa killed the Indians, cried the tenant man in chapter 5, twice. And then the third time: "We'll get our guns, like Grampa when the Indians came." A century before the composition of *Grapes*, in the winter of 1838–39, members of the Cherokee Nation made their slow, hungry way across Georgia, Tennessee, Kentucky, Illinois, Missouri, Arkansas, and into Oklahoma, settling in what came to be called Indian Territory—a trail that wound along the Arkansas River near Sallisaw. Dispossessed of their homelands, like the Joads, Cherokees rode and walked west on the "Trail of Tears." Fifty years later, what had been set aside as Indian Territory for the Cherokee and other Southeastern tribes was opened to white settlers, "Boomers," who lined up at the territorial border to claim a piece of what was called the "last frontier"; settlers could claim 160 acres of Indian Territory or "unclaimed land" near the Oklahoma panhandle. Earlier, some of that Cherokee land had been given to displaced western Indian tribes relocated to Oklahoma after the Civil War. And before the war, slaves had been brought to Oklahoma who, when freed, worked as sharecroppers on former cotton plantations. The Joads once owned 40 acres, perhaps purchased from some of the freed slaves in Oklahoma or perhaps from the Cherokee, who sold some of their land when it was legal to do so.

I don't think that Steinbeck was ignorant of this complex history of land ownership and displacement. He had a map before him as he wrote. He was a prodigious reader of history. Muley Graves says that his father had been in Oklahoma for fifty years, precisely the date of the 1889 land rush to Indian Territory. And while Steinbeck may not have been to eastern Oklahoma before he wrote *The Grapes of Wrath*—his movements during two years of research are not at all clear since he kept his research under wraps—he would certainly have learned something about the Joads' homeland before the family begins traveling its own trail of tears to California.

Histories tend to repeat themselves. The Cherokee were displaced and then displaced again, their story not unlike the Joads'.

In manuscript, Tom Joad has Indian blood: his eyes were "very dark brown and there was a hint of brown pigment on his eyeballs that usually means some Indian blood." Steinbeck crossed out the last phrase. Although it seems that he briefly intended to link Tom's history more forcefully with the Cherokee saga, he didn't do so. In this novel, Steinbeck's warp was clearly the story of white Southwestern migrants because whiteness was the gauntlet he threw down to the Associated Farmers. In effect this novel says to the powerful: Oklahoma migrants are just like you, just as land hungry, with the same Protestant heritage and they are not going to be excluded from California by legal decree as were the Japanese and the Chinese before them.

Indians are referenced again in the interchapter 23: "They was a brave on a ridge, against the sun." A figure against the sky is an iconic image in America fiction: James Fenimore Cooper's wilderness scout, Natty Bumppo, etched against a sunset prairie, is "colossal," "musing," and "melancholy." Elevating the status of equally heroic pioneers, Willa Cather, one of Carol Steinbeck's favorite writers, put a plow against a setting sun. And Steinbeck poses an Indian brave, naked and "arms spread out like a cross." When the soldiers reluctantly kill the brave, under orders, the storyteller feels that he has "spoiled somepin in haself, an' you can't never fix it up." These melancholy symbols all remind readers of something lost in the American west, some image of ourselves as Americans that cannot be recovered: Natty's pristine wilderness, Cather's Jeffersonian pioneers, and Steinbeck's spiritual connection to place, so palpable in his second novel, *To a God Unknown*. The Indian "looked big—as God," and in murdering the Indian, what have the soldiers accomplished in clearing the land?

This novel starts and ends with land misused by man: Oklahoma sharecroppers exhaust the soil and California owners waste the soil's bounty by dumping potatoes in a river and burning piles of oranges to keep prices high—"a crime that goes beyond denunciation," Steinbeck insists in chapter 25. The displaced Indian is part of that crime. In *The Grapes of Wrath*, Steinbeck implicates white America in land abuse, be it Oklahoma sharecroppers who keep planting cotton, ignore the land's natural contours, and exhaust the soil; or California growers who refuse workers decent wages and focus on profits from their crops; or soldiers who clear the land of the native peoples. From Oklahoma to California, the land has been violated: "The world is furrowed and cut, torn and blasted by man," Steinbeck writes in *Sea of Cortez*. "His desire has created that technical ability. . . . He is the only animal who lives outside of himself, whose drive is in external things—property, houses, money, concepts of power." And if that process means that God or spirit is sacrificed, as seems the implication in the story about the Indian on the ridge, then what ethical connection to land have Americans also sacrificed?

It's a question embedded in this novel.

Other histories resonate in *The Grapes of Wrath*—border tensions for one. In Arizona a guard tells them to "keep movin'." In Needles, by the Colorado River and the California border, Ma is told, "We don't want you goddamn Okies settlin' down," and a final slur is thrown after they stop for gas: "Them goddamn Okies got no sense and no feeling. They ain't human." At the Daggett inspection station, the guards look in at dead Granma, and Ma shrinks in terror at the laws they represent. Borders are contested and fearful ground in this book.

For a few weeks in early 1936, the Los Angeles Police

Department, on its own initiative, threw up a blockade across the California-Arizona border, the "bum blockade," which prevented migrants from crossing into California. At sixteen major points along the Arizona, Nevada, and Oregon borders, over 100 police officers stopped hitchhikers and "all other persons who have no definite purpose in coming into the state," as the *Los Angeles Times* reported. In liberal reformer Lincoln Steffens's eyes, the police action was "the clearest Nazi and lawless action yet perpetrated by law officials in California." It lasted two months.

Once in California, migrants found "a Hooverville on the edge of every town." In Salinas it was called Little Oklahoma, later Alisal. But in most towns, "always they were called Hooverville." They were shantytowns, patched together of corrugated iron and cardboard and tin, named after President Herbert Hoover, who many Americans thought bore responsibility for the Depression.

"Once California belonged to Mexico," chapter 19 begins. First Spanish and then Mexican land grants of the eighteenth and nineteenth centuries gave individuals enormous tracts of thousands of acres, used for cattle grazing (as any reader of Richard Henry Dana's *Two Years Before the Mast* knows). In Monterey County, Steinbeck's home turf, there were twelve of these grants, all cultivable land. In *Grapes*, William Randolph Hearst signifies this history, a man who owns a huge swath of California unimaginable to the Joads ("They's a fella, newspaper fella near the coast, got a million acres—" a man tells Casy and Tom at the Colorado River. "Casy demanded, 'What in hell can he do with a million acres?'"). Carol Steinbeck, a writer of jaunty verse, had this to say about Hearst, outlandish sentiments that her husband no doubt shared:

> Mr. Hearst has no soul.
> I hope he falls down into a hole.
> I wouldn't touch Mr. Hearst with a ten-foot pole.
> He makes me sick.
> . . .
> Mr. Hearst is a phony.
> His newspapers are full of baloney.
> I hope he loses all his moany, money
> And starves to death.
> I've got no use for this cheap skater.
> I hope he breaks his neck on a potater,
> And nobody finds it out until nine months later,
> Or never.

In the twenty-first century, it may seem easy to shrug off the historical patina of *Grapes*, brief references to Indians or the bum patrol or Hoovervilles or Mr. Hearst. But each historical referent is a part of the greater whole. Each is like the broken piece of coral that either matters as part of American history or not. Borders made impregnable, so that the barbarians don't cross into "our" land. The poor huddled in enclaves at the edges of towns. Wealth clutched in one man's hand. Such are frightening realities—then and now.

CHAPTER 17

MIGRANTS

◆ ◆ ◆

THE WORD MIGRANT is slippery. The first definition is a person or an animal that moves from one place, region, or country to another. A *National Geographic* handout geared for sixth to eighth graders amplifies the meaning to movements of people from one place to another, suggesting semipermanent or permanent residency. Semipermanent residence is, for example, a farmworker, the lesson notes. Migrant workers are thus temporary, not permanent, residents. To include both possibilities in the definition of migration embeds tension in the notion of migrant workers. Are they workers intending to move on or workers intending to stay?

Carey McWilliams was a man on the ground in the 1930s, and he later wrote about a theme that, he insisted, had been largely ignored in discussions of *The Grapes of Wrath*: "The dust bowl migration seemed to mark a climactic moment in the century-old saga of migratory farm labor in California." When farm prices fell in the early 1930s, Mexicans were "ousted" in "special deportation trains, as one might ship cattle from one point to another." Then the Okies came and "for the first time in history" the farm labor force in California "was made up, in about equal parts, of aliens and native-born Americans. It seemed, therefore, that with the arrival of the Joads, the jig was up for the big growers. . . . In a word, the historical cycle of migration to the West coincided with what appeared to be the end of a cycle in the history of migratory farm labor."

The Joads are part of a *migration*—they were in California to stay, while the Chinese, Japanese, Filipino, and Mexican field-workers were *migratory* and thus deportable.

The border guard at Arizona tells the Joads: "Go ahead, but you better keep movin'." Migrants staying put in a little white house doesn't go down well, then and now.

Sis Cunningham, born in Oklahoma in 1909, wrote the song "How Can You Keep On Movin'" about Oklahoma migrants, recorded by the New Lost City Ramblers in 1959 and by Ry Cooder in the 1970s. It articulates precisely this tension:

> *How can you keep on movin' (unless you*
> *migrate too)*
> *They tell ya to keep on movin' but migrate, you*
> *must not do*

> *The only reason for movin' and the reason why*
> *   I roam*
> *To move to a new location and find myself a home*

Uncle John asks Al near the end of the book, "Know where we're a-goin'?" And Al responds, "No . . . Jus' goin', an gettin' goddamn sick of it."

CHAPTER 18

"CARE LIKE HELL."

❖ ❖ ❖

AT THE CLIMAX of the Joads' trek, as they roll into the
Weedpatch camp, another history is embedded in this
novel: California's camp program, a federal government
initiative to provide temporary, safe, and sanitary housing for migrant field-workers in a number of communities around the state. Writing newspaper articles about
this program propelled Steinbeck into what he called his
"four pound book" in the fall of 1936.

One of Steinbeck's college friends insisted that John
was a journalist at heart, a writer itching to be on the
scene, see for himself, listen to dialogue, discover detail.
During his forty-year career, John Steinbeck wrote nearly
as much nonfiction as fiction, and scores of articles and
essays appeared in newspapers and magazines. (His journalism is collected in *"America and Americans" and Selected Nonfiction* [2002], and his World War II and
Vietnam dispatches have been collected and reissued as

Once There Was a War [1958] and *Steinbeck in Vietnam* [2012].) And he published longer nonfiction works—*Sea of Cortez* (1941), *A Russian Journal* (1948), *Travels with Charley* (1962), and *America and Americans* (1966). One of his first jobs after he left Stanford University in 1925, without taking a degree, was as a journalist in New York City. "I didn't know the first thing about being a reporter," he admitted later in an essay called "Making of a New Yorker." He failed at beat reporting, since he embellished stories with fictive flourishes—for which he was fired. He fled back to California. New York had "beaten the pants off me."

By the time of his next journalistic assignment in the late summer of 1936, he was far more seasoned. He had published five novels, written six, and his prose over that decade had become sturdier, more sinewy. The *San Francisco News*, fiercely liberal, hired the now well-known John Steinbeck to write articles on migrant housing in California. "The Harvest Gypsies" series, published in 1936, byline John Steinbeck, and with accompanying photos by Dorothea Lange, is the taproot of *The Grapes of Wrath*.

His was a somewhat reluctant transformation into firebrand. During the first half of the 1930s, Steinbeck had written steadily and well about the people he knew in Monterey County: ranchers, farmers, a dredging foreman, paisanos. His parents' deaths in 1934 and 1935 put a psychic boundary to that phase of his career—they had supported their son's quest to be a writer and he had, in the end, proved worthy. Mid-decade, financially secure with the publication of *Tortilla Flat* in 1935, Steinbeck was primed for new material—labor unrest in California.

Both his wife, Carol, and his radical neighbor in Carmel, journalist Lincoln Steffens, urged him to get involved. "Care like hell," Steffens had told muckraking journalists at the turn of the century, and he probably said about the same to Steinbeck and the other young writers who visited the aging radical at his home in Carmel during the early 1930s. Steffens and his wife, Ella Winter, edited a socialist newspaper in Carmel, the *Pacific Weekly*, and were members of the John Reed Club, a clutch of Communists thirty or so strong. Although Winter was an ardent Communist and Steffens was not a member of the party, Steffens nonetheless believed that Communists would lead workers and the dispossessed to socialism, a new order. He championed Robert Cantwell's 1934 novel about a labor strike in Northwest logging country, *The Land of Plenty* (1934), as a "new kind of fiction" about a strike "without a hero and without a villain."

But neutrality was not typical of the 1930s, when ideological warfare between conservative growers and radical unionists was intense, protracted, and sometimes violent. Workers were caught in the middle of perpetual debates between capitalism and collectivism.

Steinbeck's first labor novel was *In Dubious Battle*, the title from Milton's *Paradise Lost*. His next book about labor was more intimate, a novella about the friendship between two workers, one angry and restless, the other pliant: George Milton and Lennie Small. Their names suggest one of Steinbeck's intentions in this little study of humility, as he called it: John Milton writ small. In *Of Mice and Men*, the "life of Man" is observed in microcosm, two workers on the road, imagining a snug home place, depending on one another for psychological and physical well-being. A home and land for George and Lennie, maybe for Candy and Crooks, is the ideal pursued (not workers uniting), a vision that is palpable throughout this novel of broken dreams. Chosen for the Book-of-the-Month Club and sent to its over 200,000 members, this novella made Steinbeck famous across America.

When he finished writing *Of Mice and Men* in July 1936, he went first to San Francisco to the offices of the Resettlement Administration Region IX, which covered Arizona, California, Nevada, and Utah, gathering data from their files. Then, in company with regional manager Eric H. Thomsen, he went to the San Joaquin Valley to see for himself.

His assignment for the *San Francisco News* was to write about housing for itinerant field-workers, the problem that, even today, California has never adequately solved. Migrant labor is needed to pick delicate crops— today, lettuce and strawberries and artichokes, most grapes and peaches. From the 1850s through the 1920s, first Chinese, then Japanese, then Filipino and Mexican workers were brought into California to fill that need for temporary labor. But where to shelter workers who are needed on a ranch only a few weeks a year? And what to do with the white migrants of the 1930s who could not so easily be shunted into invisible places, who believed that migration ended with a permanent home?

By 1936, the lack of housing had become more acute as thousands of displaced farmers from the Southwest poured into California, drawn by the promise of orange groves and sun, the promotional images that the railroads had popularized across America. Witnesses from the 1930s claim that growers advertised for workers in the Dust Bowl states—certainly Steinbeck said they did so, as did his friend Tom Collins and Carey McWilliams, who wrote an equally searing account of the workers' woe, *Factories in the Field*. (Kevin Starr, author of a multivolume history of California, claims that growers did not circulate handbills outside the state, that he never found one in any California archive. Why would growers do that, the argument goes, when the state was chockablock with workers, far more than needed? I still believe Steinbeck and Collins and McWilliams, all of whom say that growers did just that.) Although many growers provided housing for the laborers they hired, some did not, and in any case the housing was inadequate for the burgeoning number of migrants. Shacks were often substandard. A toilet might be shared by fifty workers, and separate male and female facilities did not exist. Communal cooking facilities were scarce. Families were crowded into one-room hovels.

For migrants forced into roadside camps, conditions were worse—water scarce, disease rampant. "Armies of migratory workers are living under conditions that would not be tolerable in pigpens," Eric Thomsen proclaimed in a speech in San Jose in the mid-1930s. In California's Central Valley, in the Salinas and Santa Clara Valleys, the fields were lined with walnuts and pears, oranges and peaches, grapes and apples, spindly lettuce and scarlet strawberries, but the land's bounty was an ironic reminder that abundance was denied to those who harvested them.

Resistance to Southwest migrants mounted steadily in the 1930s. Hospitals and schools could not accommodate the swelling migrant population in rural areas. And the newcomers seemed strange to locals: Okies drawled their words and tended to be fervent Christians, singing and shouting and praying. A health official in Fresno declared that migrants were "incapable of being absorbed into our civilization." He continued his speech: "You cannot legislate these people out of California . . . but you can make it difficult for them when they are here." This is pretty much the theme of today's efforts to make unregistered aliens "self-deport."

In 1935, responding to appeals by Californians for assistance with the migrant surge, the federal government provided money for sanitary and safe migrant housing, with some local governments signing on as well. Getting the camps built, however, was "uphill every inch of the way," Helen Hosmer recalled. The first two government camps were built in Marysville (dedicated on October 5, 1935) and in Arvin, at the southern end of the Central Valley (Weedpatch in the novel). The camp that Jim Rawley manages is an oasis for the Joads—as it was for many migrants, who were treated with the same dignity that the Joads received. But some local residents and certainly growers resented these government camps in their communities, fearing that they would attract Communist organizers. When Tom Collins bought land for a camp in Brawley in 1937, an editorial noted that "the hammer and sickle would soon be hoisted on the very rim of town." And as Collins's crew built tent platforms for the Brawley camp, the Parent-Teacher Association arrived:

"Are you going to make it possible for more of these hobo brats to go to school with our children?" The Associated Farmers of Brawley weighed in, the county supervisor declaring, "We never wanted this camp in here. White men are no good in our business. We like our Mexicans. They don't complain; they live where we put them, and they aren't forever organizing. . . ." The camps were "hotbeds of communism," in growers' eyes. One camp manager was greeted at the Yuba City camp with an editorial calling him "Comrade Iusi." Farmers were "blackballing" Okies who lived in the camps, he recalled.

In mid-1936, the *San Francisco News* hoped that balanced, sympathetic reporting by Steinbeck would squelch similar vitriol.

Steinbeck and Eric Thomsen arrived at the second of the fifteen camps to be constructed, the Arvin camp four miles south of Bakersfield, often called Weedpatch for the nearest small town. A twenty-acre tract had been divided into twelve blocks with eight tent sites in each. The camp could accommodate ninety-six families, and overseeing the families and the operation was gentle and compassionate Tom Collins, manager of the first few government camps:

> The first time I saw [Tom Collins] it was evening, and it was raining. I drove into the migrant camp, the wheels of my car throwing muddy water. The lines of sodden, dripping tents stretched away from me in the darkness. The temporary office was crowded with damp men and women, just standing under a roof, and sitting at a littered ta-

ble was [Collins], a little man in a damp, frayed
white suit. The crowding people looked at him all
the time. Just stood and looked at him. He had a
small moustache, his graying, black hair stood up
on his head like the quills of a frightened porcu-
pine, and his large, dark eyes, tired beyond sleep-
iness, the kind of tired that won't let you sleep
even if you have time and a bed.

As director, Collins organized migrants into self-
governing units and then provided recreational, sanitary,
and child welfare programs to "re-Americanize" them,
"building up of a morale and better citizenship and a
feeling of better security and contentment and the like—
with the subsistence farm as an integral part of the program here at Kern." Collins wanted to create a democratic
community. As his Arvin camp drew national attention
to the housing issue, he started a school to train other
managers—five new camps were soon scheduled after
success at Arvin was demonstrated.

Then and later, touring other makeshift "squatter
camps" where the destitute huddled, Steinbeck and Thomsen and Collins "sat in the ditches with the migrant workers, lived and ate with them. . . . We ate fried dough and sow
belly, worked with the sick and the hungry, listened to complaints and little triumphs." Tom Collins would be Steinbeck's point person for the next two years, and he would
come to share with Carol the dedication for *The Grapes
of Wrath*: "To Carol who willed this book. To Tom who
lived it."

Steinbeck read Collins's finely tuned weekly reports

that he sent to the Resettlement Administration office in San Francisco, pages filled with statistics, commentary on wages and conditions, "migrant wisdom," scraps of conversation, lyrics of Okie ballads—an eclectic mix of migrant lore. Those reports, Steinbeck's on-site tours with Collins around Kern County, and his own experience with growers and shippers in Salinas would form the backbone of the articles that appeared in the *San Francisco News* in October 1936.

In "Squatters' Camps," the third in the series, Steinbeck invites readers to participate, to see "on close approach" how families live. "Here is a house built by a family, who have tried to maintain a neatness," he begins, sketching a "ten feet by ten feet" house of "corrugated paper." The tour continues: "There is more filth here." And "Here, in the faces of the husband and wife, you begin to see an expression you will notice on every face; not worry, but absolute terror of the starvation that crowds in against the borders of the camp." The prose is straightforward, composed of simple sentences detailing visual evidence. He pulls no punches. "I have described three typical families," he concludes. "Some are so far from water that it must be bought at five cents a bucket." And his editorial comment is limited to a single sentence that closes the article: "And if these men steal, if there is developing among them a suspicion and hatred of well-dressed, satisfied people, the reason is not to be sought in their origin nor in any tendency to weakness in their character."

The pleasure of reading Steinbeck's journalism is its immediacy and clarity, sometimes its humor, here its sharp anger.

There were seven of these articles. In 1938, the seven plus one additional essay, "Starvation Under the Orange Trees," were published as *Their Blood Is Strong*, a booklet from the Simon J. Lubin Society which cost twenty-five cents, sold out quickly, and was reprinted four times.

The Arvin-Weedpatch camp still exists, now called the Sunset Camp. In 2001, the Lamott Historical Society raised $500,000 to restore three of the original 1935 buildings: the community center, the library, and the post office. In 2002, one hundred stucco houses replaced thirty-year-old temporary housing. It is one of twenty-six Migrant Family Housing Centers run by the state of California, available to agricultural workers who depend on agricultural employment for at least 50 percent of their total annual household income and do not live within a fifty-mile radius of the housing center. They are open half the year, from April to October or November.

CHAPTER 19

BEYOND THE JOAD NICHE

◆ ◆ ◆

A YEAR AFTER *The Grapes of Wrath* was published, Steinbeck worked on two Mexican projects: the book *Sea of Cortez* and a documentary film called *The Forgotten Village*, about a cholera epidemic in a small Mexican village. He wrote a preface to the latter that clarifies the structure of that film:

> Our story centered on one family in one small village. We wished our audience to know this family very well, and incidentally to like it, as we did. Then, from association with this little personalized group, the larger conclusion concerning the racial group could be drawn with something like participation. Birth and death, joy and sorrow, are constants, experiences common to the whole species. If one participates first in these

constants, one is able to go from them to the vari-
ables of customs, practices, mores, taboos, and
foreign patterns.

Those same words apply to *The Grapes of Wrath*, a
novel that focuses on one family, the Joads, and then
moves through experiences that are common to the
whole species, past and present.

At Stanford University, where he enrolled in 1919,
Steinbeck audited (several times) world history taught by
Harold Chapman Brown, whose lectures surely imprint
The Grapes of Wrath: "What if some time an army of
them marches on the land as the Lombards did in Italy,
as the Germans did on Gaul and the Turks did on By-
zantium." That sentence in chapter 19 echoes Dr. Brown's
lectures. For Steinbeck, the Joads are a twentieth-century
equivalent of the "land-hungry, ill-armed hordes." And
for many Californians, migrants like the Joads were
barbarians.

In several ways, the Joads' story is universal—and the
novel's insistent metaphorical reach defines layer four.

Eight years ago, I met one of Steinbeck's Stanford
friends, Bob Cathcart, at a book launch. I had interviewed Bob a few years earlier, when, in his late eighties,
he was still practicing law in San Francisco. By then in
his midnineties, Bob invited me several times to his San
Francisco home for lunch, where he would tell me about
John and his reading habits. His memory was prodigious.
John checked out the *Hermetica* of Trismegistus from the
Stanford library several times, Bob said. This book on the
religious and philosophical teachings of the Greeks fasci-

nated him. In the late 1920s, Bob lent John his copy of Herodotus—and never got it back. Still a classicist, Bob lent me tapes from the Teaching Company about Greek myths, and I gave him mine about Athens in the golden age. This is my one-degree-of-separation story, but also I cannot consider Steinbeck's keen interest in ancient history without a nod to gracious Bob Cathcart,

The niches that the Joads occupy—Oklahoma share-croppers, Okie migrants, California field-workers—are linked to niches across space and time, universal and mythic histories of land use, dispossession, and poverty. The Joads' land hunger is the land hunger of many. Only one passage was dropped from the manuscript by the Viking Press—and it was probably something else Stein-beck learned from Professor Chapman Brown's lectures. The omitted passage is 160 words from chapter 19, an interchapter about California's hostility toward migrants:

> Once the Germans in their hordes came to the rich margin of Rome, and they came timidly, say-ing we have been driven, give us land. And the Romans armed the frontier and built forts against the hordes of needs. And the legions patrolled the borders, cased in metal, armed with the best steel. And the barbarians came naked across the border—humbly, humbly. They received the swords in their breasts and marched on, and their dead bore down the swords and the barbarians marched on and took the land. And they were driven by their need, and they conquered with their need. In battle the women fought in the line

and the yellow haired children lay in the grass with knives to hamstring the legionnaires, to snick through the hamstrings of the horses. But the legions had no needs, no wills, no force. And the best trained, best armed troops in the world went down before the hordes of need.

The resolute and hungry survive, while the heavily armored, the great owners with too much land, fall. There are the "three cries of history," Steinbeck writes in chapter 19: when land is in too few hands it is taken away; when the masses are hungry and cold, they take what they need; when the people are repressed, they grow stronger. Steinbeck's historicism is laid out in that impassioned chapter. Surfeit makes people soft and vulnerable. Survivability, a concept that he and Ricketts discussed at length, was a trait of the struggling, not the satiated. Like the barbarians, the Joads had a higher "survivability quotient," in Ricketts's words, because they were land hungry and hardworking and adaptable.

Maybe the editors wanted Steinbeck to cut that paragraph, essentially repetitious, because he clarified Professor Chapman Brown's lessons so very well in the rest of chapter 19. Dispossession and yearning for land are universal niches, occurring and recurring everywhere.

The Grapes of Wrath, a little like *Moby Dick* in this respect, keeps starting over, circling back to the primal scenes of land loss and land hunger. After Tom and Al have fixed the Wilsons' broken car, for example, they rejoin the family at a roadside camp. Like the earlier overnight campout with Casy, Tom, and Muley, this scene assembles key figures in a drama of dispossession: those in power (deputy sheriff and proprietor); those who have lost a home (Pa and a young man); and a soothsayer (the "ragged man"). At the roadside camp Pa mourns the loss of land: "It's dirt hard for folks to tear up an' go. Folks like us that had our place. We ain't shif'less. Till we got tractored off, we was people with a farm." A young man asks if they were sharecroppers. "Sure we was sharcroppin'," Pa replies. "Use' ta own the place."

The young man faced forward again. "Same as us," he said.

"Lucky for us it ain't gonna las' long," said Pa. "We'll get out west an' we'll get work an' we'll get a piece a grown' land with water."

The Joads, like Muley and the young man, are farmers spiraling downward—from landowners, to croppers, to migrants, a replicated history of displacement. It's important that the Joads owned land, since land ownership lends authority to their saga, land loss dignity to their story. Land loss is one mythic story told here; and land imagined, fecund, and well watered is the other. "The loss of home became one loss," Steinbeck writes about people on the road, "and the golden time in the West was one dream." There is no clear end point to the story Steinbeck tells—no land for the Joads, no food, no home. But the searing loss and unquenchable yearning is refigured over and over in this novel.

When the Joads stop by the Colorado River, yet another soothsayer appears, a sun-bitten father who has been to California and is now going back home. Power is embodied in the "newspaper fella near the coast," William Randolph Hearst, who "got a million acres"—a clear case of land greed. And Uncle John is the realist: "None of this here talk gonna keep us from goin' there."

"Soon's we can, I want a little house," Ma reiterates in the government camp.

Nothing in American (and world) history is more urgent and compelling than that hunger for land, the dream of self-sufficiency—as this book reiterates and replicates, voices and preaches and dramatizes. It's the Jeffersonian idyll of cultivating a small farm. It's the pioneer saga and the doctrine of Manifest Destiny. It's an Oklahoma story about the "Boomers" of 1889, and it's a California story of the vast Spanish and Mexican land grants. It's an ecological story as well, about land "gullied up" because the contours were ignored by settlers and about land depleted by one water-thirsty crop, cotton. And it's an immigrant story. The urgency of that land hunger and desire for self-sufficiency reaches beyond the boundaries of white America and the 1930s.

Land loss, land use, and an imagined acreage is hardly confined to American shores. To paraphrase Joseph Campbell, whom Steinbeck befriended briefly in 1932, land ownership is the story with a thousand faces. One version of that story is the barbarian hordes on the Roman borders. We had land once and we will have it again.

Some of the punch that *The Grapes of Wrath* delivers is in the insistence and relevance of that story.

The first Steinbeck Chair of the National Steinbeck Center in Salinas, in 2003–04, was Victor Villaseñor, author of *Rain of Gold*, who voiced a Mexican version:

When I read his book, *To a God Unknown*, was when Steinbeck just ripped me out of my life and took me someplace that I have never been taken by another author. He loved the land, and I grew up with my father talking about Los Altos de Jalisco and how it was a mythical place. So my father had always talked about the land and ranching with such reverence—that we were connected to the land. Steinbeck wrote with such a love for this land, for this property.

Other niches also lift the Joad story from the 1930s to the present—land use and sustainability, oppression and prejudice.

To love the land is to know it and work it and harvest its bounty. *The Grapes of Wrath* is about agriculture, and humans' relation to what they grow and consume. This novel reminds us, or should, to know something about local food production, to recognize, for example, something similar to what Steinbeck knew about his home turf: that artichokes start the Salinas Valley season in March, with several artichokes cut from each plant, followed by strawberries (several pickings) and then lettuce. Broccoli and cauliflower are year-round crops but most often planted during rainy Salinas winters. This novel reminds us that agriculture is a business, large and profitable, the "largest driver of Monterey County's economy." In 2012, crop values were $4.4 billion, a record-breaking year, with leaf lettuce the most profitable crop. Strawberries are also on the top of the list, with

88 percent of U.S. strawberries coming from this area. Spinach is making a comeback.

This novel reminds us of the interconnections of soil, labor, housing, energy, water, rain, and the time of the harvest and what crops grow where. And of course, this novel reminds us of the ways that global warming changes everything.

And yet another niche is that oppression is a constant of the species, as searing in 1939 as it was in the last decade of Steinbeck's life, the 1960s, and as it is today. Steinbeck never ceased to consider the terrible legacy of oppression, a niche across time.

In July 1964, shortly after the passage of the Civil Rights Act, Steinbeck wrote to Martin Luther King Jr. about the history of racism: "When one man outrages another he must justify it to himself with the conviction that his victim is/was evil, unworthy or inferior." That, he knew, was how Californians had responded to Okies. But in the present moment, 1964, Steinbeck fears what the rioting in Harlem will bring: "It is of greatest importance, particularly in the months to come before the Presidential election, that the discipline of Negros by themselves and the dignity that they have achieved be reestablished in the public mind." Steinbeck counseled restraint.

A year later, screenwriter Budd Schulberg brought Steinbeck an autographed book entitled *From the Ashes* from his Watts Writers Workshop, a project that grew out of the 1965 Watts riots. Steinbeck read the collection with great interest. "I tell you something" about these young black writers, he said to Budd. "I know they're angry and feel on the bottom that they've got nothing because we took it all—but I envy those young writers. . . . They don't have to search for material. They're living it every day. The subject matter is built-in dynamite. There's no luxury quite like having something to say."

His comments about race are hardly consistent, advising caution on the one hand, praising action on the other, and yet the letters say something important about John Steinbeck's rugged, kind, and curious soul. He was in it to the end, assessing America's people, empathizing with the disenfranchised from the 1930s through the 1960s.

"From the first we have treated our minorities abominably," he would write in 1966, in his last publication, *America and Americans*, a jeremiad for his countrymen, written a quarter century after his magnum opus, *The Grapes of Wrath*:

> All that was required to release this mechanism of oppression and sadism was that the newcomers be meek, poor, weak in numbers, and unprotected— although it helped if their skin, hair, eyes were different and if they spoke some language other than English or worshiped in some church other than Protestant. The Pilgrim Fathers took out after the Catholics, and both clobbered the Jews. The Irish had their turn running the gantlet, and after them the Germans, the Poles, the Slovaks, the Italians, the Hindus, the Chinese, the Japanese, the Filipinos, the Mexicans. To all these people we gave disparaging names . . .

In the 1930s that name was "Okies," a name that meant to many Californians the shiftless, dirty, and illiterate and unwanted poor. "These goddamned Okies are dirty and ignorant," Steinbeck writes in the anonymous speech of interchapters, mimicking Californians' resistance to newcomers. "They're degenerate, sexual maniacs. These goddamned Okies are thieves. They'll steal anything."

That's not very different from the racial slurs that white "cheerleaders" hurl at a black child trying to attend school, the bleakest passage in Steinbeck's other American journey, *Travels with Charley* (1962). America struggles with names that have ugly histories, bloody consequences. In its universal implications, *The Grapes of Wrath* says something urgent and sadly true about marginalized Americans, workers and minorities of all colors.

In short, Ricketts's notion of recurring niches, his fourth layer of ecological study, honeycombs *The Grapes of Wrath*. The novel insistently moves from particular to general—to universals. Steinbeck embeds a skein of associations that ties this book to other stories, other issues, other myths. Much of the commentary on *The Grapes of Wrath* has scrutinized all these mythic parallels, to good ends: The Joads are like the Israelites seeking the Promised Land in Exodus. The Joads are like Everyman, trudging through a sinful world and believing in a better place. The Joads are like Odysseus, yearning for home. Casy is Christlike and also channels the best of Whitman and Blake and Emerson. Tom is "Jesus Meek," another kind of savior in the book. Ma is the archetypal mother and caregiver. As biographer Jackson Benson notes, Steinbeck drew from anthropologist Robert Briffault's three-volume study *The Mothers* (1927), which traces the importance of matriarchy across cultures: "All tender feelings, and altruism in the male, must have arisen through maternal love, and through the transference of these instincts to the male. Therefore these sentiments and social virtues which are necessary to the existence of any form of human society have their original root in the feeling which characterizes the relation between mother and offspring." Ma's nurturing of both Tom and Rose of Sharon is not only at the heart of *The Grapes of Wrath*, but true across cultures, according to Briffault.

Rose of Sharon, her name from the Song of Songs ("I am the rose of Sharon, and the lily of the valleys"), is another archetype. And her final gesture, notes classicist Joseph Fontenrose, is ritualistic, common in "primitive adoption rituals [where] the adopting mother offers her breast to the adopted child." Since Rose of Sharon cannot be a mother, she "adopts the newly born collective person as represented by one of 'the people'" who huddle together in the barn, and thus conveys to the larger unit the "unity and strength" of the family bond.

Readers come back to *The Grapes of Wrath* because it captures what is "eternal to our species."

Another passage from *Sea of Cortez* that I love gracefully explains that external spirit—and Steinbeck's notion of niches. When the crew visits Loreto, they are struck by the lovely statue of Our Lady of Loreto at the Loreto mission. She is

> one of the strong ecological factors of the town of Loreto, and not to know her and her strength

is to fail to know Loreto. . . . [T]his plaster lady [has] a powerful effect on the deep black water of the human spirit. She may disappear and her name be lost, as the Magna Mater, as Isis, have disappeared. But something very like her will take her place, and the longings which created her will find somewhere in the world a similar altar on which to pour their force. No matter what her name is, Artemis, or Venus, or a girl behind a Woolworth counter vaguely remembered, she is as eternal as our species, and we will continue to manufacture her as long as we survive.

ſyſtemic ſins

♦ ♦ ♦

Another niche.

At the beginning of the novel, the former preacher Jim Casy tells Tom that while in the wilderness he rejected a Christian notion of sin: "There ain't no sin and there ain't no virtue," Casy insists when the two first meet. "There's just stuff people do. It's all part of the same thing. And some of the things folks do is nice, and some ain't nice, but that's as far as any man got a right to say." Casy "preaches" this nonjudgmental position to guilt-ridden Uncle John, who is consumed by what he believes to be his sin—letting his wife die. And there are other references to sin in this book. In the government camp, Mrs. Sandry is dead certain what constitutes sin: the theater and "clutch-an'-hug" dancing. All this talk of sin focuses on the individual, the stuff people do.

But this novel reconfigures the meaning of sin more

than once, moving from personal to systemic sins. Crimes that go "beyond denunciation" are systemic, not individual: when oranges are burned to keep prices high, "the smell of rot fills the country"—the message of chapter 25. Camp manager Jim Rawley "don' believe in sin," Mrs. Sandry tells Rose of Sharon; he says, she sniffs, that "sin is being hungry" and people being cold. That's a notion of sin Mrs. Sandry cannot possibly grasp. But Casy can—and when he reunites with Tom near the end of the book, he schools Tom in his own, revitalized sense of wrongdoing. Casy has moved from detached tolerance to full-throated engagement and tells Tom: "Here's me, been a-goin' into the wilderness like Jesus to try find out somepin. Almost got her sometimes, too. But it's in the jail house I really got her." What he got is the big picture: "It's need that makes all the trouble," he tells a baffled Tom—need for food and housing and good wages and a decent life. Casy and Jim Rawley voice the same notion of systemic sins—and by the time Tom bids his final farewell to Ma, he has come to a similar conclusion.

Commitment is the response to systemic failures, the only "solution" this book embraces—in the actions of Jim and Casy and Tom, in the sensibilities of Ma and Rose of Sharon. "Somewhere I saw the criticism that this book was anti-religious," Eleanor Roosevelt wrote in her syndicated column, "My Day," in June 1939. "But somehow I cannot imagine thinking of 'Ma Joad' without, at the same time, thinking of the love 'that passeth all understanding.' It's a profoundly religious, spiritual, and ethically urgent book."

I once asked Elaine Steinbeck, John's third wife,

about his religious sentiments, and she responded that he had a spiritual streak: "There was always a spiritual quality to John . . . he did not feel that he had to go to church on Sunday; he didn't. But when he went, he acted like an active church goer." Most certainly, the lovely, tangled, and fragile world of nature is Steinbeck's window to the intangible. In the early 1930s he wrote that "the stones, the trees, the muscled mountains are the world—but not the world apart from man—the world and man—the one indescribable unit man plus his environment." Awareness of interdependence, properly attended, opens to spirit.

Those like Mrs. Sandry, self-righteous and bitter and cruel, close themselves to nature and to human suffering. Those who embrace both the joy and agony of our species are beacons, bringers of light, like Jim Rawley, like Casy, like Ma. The man in jail tells Casy that "Ever' time they's a little step fo'ward, she may slip back a little, but she never slips clear back. You can prove that, an' that makes the whole thing right."

As World War II loomed, Steinbeck said something similar to his editor, Pat Covici:

> Maybe you can find some vague theology that will give you hope. Not that I have lost any hope. All the goodness and heroisms will rise up again, then be cut down again and rise up. It isn't that the evil thing wins—it never will—but that it doesn't die.

And in *Sea of Cortez* Steinbeck reiterates Casy's ideas about interconnectedness and spiritual yearning:

Man is related to the whole thing, related inextricably to all reality, known as unknowable. This is a simple thing to say, but the profound feeling of it made a Jesus, a St. Augustine, a St. Francis, a Roger Bacon, a Charles Darwin, and an Einstein. Each of them in his own tempo and with his own voice discovered and reaffirmed with astonishment that all things are one thing and that one thing is all things—plankton, a shimmering phosphorescence of the sea and the spinning planets and an expanding universe, all bound together by the elastic string of time.

That passage speaks to layer four—universal ideas—and leads to layer five—emergence.

CHAPTER 21

MA TO TOM: "EVER'THING
YOU DO IS MORE'N YOU."

❖ ❖ ❖

AFTER A MONTH of writing, Steinbeck finished what he saw as book I, chapters 1–11, and wrote in his journal: "I went over the whole of the book in my head—fixed on the last scene, huge and symbolic, toward which the whole story moves." He was writing toward layer five, the emergent ending, the ending that readers either love or hate.

Steinbeck's first readers hated it.

In early January 1939, Viking editors sat down for a joint editorial report on the manuscript that, by that time, all had read. Harold Guinzburg, the president of Viking Press, said he wouldn't change a "single comma in the whole book," and Marshall Best, the managing editor, was equally enthusiastic about the novel that had left all of them "emotionally exhausted." Although excited, they were also nervous, hardly surprising considering the magnitude of the project. Scores of agents around the country had been provided with salesman dummies, a popular teaser of the time. A few pages of the novel were printed; the remaining pages were blank and the "text" was bound to suggest the heft of the forthcoming book. Anticipation ran high. John Steinbeck was a red-hot property, the subject was incendiary and urgent, the novel was expected to be a blockbuster.

But the editorial team had a couple of serious reservations. On occasion, the language was obscene—they sent Steinbeck's agent west to help take care of that, snip some offending words. And in their eyes, the conclusion, although "poignant," struck a sour note. It fell to Pat Covici to inform Steinbeck of their qualms about the ending, which he did in a delicately worded missive. Considering Rose of Sharon giving her breast to a stranger in the concluding scene, he wrote,

> . . . struck us on reflection as being all too abrupt and, as our advertising man would say, "not quite satisfying as a piece of fiction." As the end of the final episode it is perfect; as the end of the whole book not quite. It seems to us that the last few pages need building up. The incident needs leading up to, so that the meeting with the starving man is not so much an accident or chance encounter, but more an integral part of the saga of the Joad family.
>
> And it needs something else leading away

from it so that the symbolism of the gesture is more apparent in relation to the book as a whole.

On the day that he received his editor's letter, January 16, 1939, an exasperated Steinbeck wrote back to say that he would not "change that ending." Rose of Sharon giving her breast to a starving man is not a "love symbol," as the editorial board seemed to think, but a "survival symbol," he wrote to Covici. The encounter

> . . . must be an accident, it must be a stranger, and it must be quick. To build this stranger into the structure of the book would be to warp the whole meaning of the book. The fact that the Joads don't know him, don't care about him, have no ties to him—that is the emphasis. The giving of the breast has no more sentiment than the giving of a piece of bread.

In that response is the keystone of this magisterial novel of social and psychological upheaval—the notion of emergence: "Whenever you have a multitude of individuals interacting with one another there often comes a moment when disorder gives way to order and something new emerges: a pattern, a decision, a structure, or a change in direction." That happens again and again in *The Grapes of Wrath*. Random interactions occur and something happens. A novel about the dispossessed, *The Grapes of Wrath* is, on the one hand, about an old order drying up—literally in the 1930s—and the people cast

out, uprooted. But the book keeps insisting on something new taking hold, an order more complex, perhaps,
but inchoate.

Chapter 14 is the heart of this novel as surely as chapter 14 is the heart of *Sea of Cortez*—there is a long meditation on Ricketts's notion of nonteleological, or "is,"
thinking. *Grapes*' chapter 14 is a meditation on emergence, the fulcrum of the book. Emergence is a large part
of why the book endures—something will happen, as yet
unknown. While flocks of birds and swarms of ants or
bees all show emergent properties, only man (I read humans), Steinbeck asserted, "emerges ahead of his accom-
plishments." That's why this book has five layers and *Sea
of Cortez* only four. Emergence, the fifth and final layer,
is the step forward taken by humans. Only "man reaches,
stumbles forward, painfully, mistakenly sometimes." Incredible courage and activism don't often make sense or
seem believable—nor does Tom's commitment or Rose
of Sharon's gesture at the end of this book. But "fear the
time when the strikes stop while the great owners live,"
fear the time that people don't do crazy, brave things. If
that time comes, humans will have stopped taking the
foolhardy steps only we can decide to make.

In fiction those steps may seem melodramatic, staged,
unconvincing (complaints about Tom's exit speech and
Rose's breast). In a news story, the steps stun us into awe
at the human condition.

The Grapes of Wrath is a sad book in its detailed intensity. But it's a great and optimistic book in its belief
in the human spirit. Of course Rose of Sharon won't save
the man. Of course hers is a gesture, not a solution. Of

course the Joads are marooned without a home, which doesn't solve any political or sociological issues raised in the book. Of course the men of the family have fled, one way or another. But a core remains, and something will happen.

The book is full of emergent ideas. In chapter 16, Casy tells Tom that "[t]hey's gonna come somepin outa all these folks goin' wes'—outa all their farms lef' lonely. They's comin' a thing that's gonna change the whole country." In chapter 25, the most incendiary in the book, destruction and possibility rub together, creating sparks. Allowing oranges to rot when migrants are starving, simply to keep prices high, angers the hungry migrants: "In the eyes of the people there is the failure; and in the eyes of the hungry there is a growing wrath. In the souls of the people the grapes of wrath are filling and growing heavy, growing heavy for the vintage." The failure is clear: capitalism has failed because self-interest and greed have trumped compassion, certainly when mounds of oranges are burned to keep prices high. And while the grapes of wrath are not yet harvested, the vintage not bottled, collective rage might make it so—revolution simmers. Change hovers.

The final scene is "no more important than any other part of the book," Steinbeck insisted, because Rose of Sharon's unanticipated gesture of kindness, a breast offered to a stranger, is of a piece with the Joads' and migrants' lives, the randomness of lived experience. Introducing the man earlier would "warp" the novel Steinbeck wrote because an orderly plot was, in effect, inimical to what this novel is all about.

In elaborating his response to his editor, Steinbeck describes his book as if it were a jigsaw puzzle:

> . . . every incident has been too carefully chosen and its weight judged and fitted. The balance is there. One other thing—I am not writing a satisfying story. I've done my darndest to rip a reader's nerves to rags. I don't want him satisfied.
>
> And one more thing—I've tried to write this book the way lives are lived, not the way books are written.

The way lives are lived, not plotted but experienced. This is a novel of growth, death, adaptation, and emergence—a book about all life.

Chapter 3 balances the ending, its placement, no doubt, just as carefully "judged and fitted" into the novel. These often-excerpted three pages are less concerned with that well-known turtle than with the phenomenon of seed dispersal, as Stephen Railton writes in a splendid essay, each seed "possessed of the anlage of movement." Anlage means germ, zygote, essence. And so each seed is a tiny sphere of potential displacement and change. And each seed is moved by chance occurrence: wind moves seeds, animals move seeds, "a man's trouser cuff or the hem of a woman's skirt" moves seeds. And so does a turtle, who clamps "one head of wild oats" by his front legs. A woman driving a sedan sees the turtle and swings right to miss it. A man driving a light truck swerves to hit the turtle, spinning off the highway. And there by the side of the road, in the dirt, "[t]he wild oat head fell out and three of the spear head seeds stuck in the ground. And as the turtle crawled on down the embankment, its shell dragged dirt over the seeds."

The word "anlage," appearing at the end of the first paragraph in the turtle chapter, was, in fact, another point of resistance for Steinbeck, its use creating a little dust storm of editorial protest. It was one of Ed Ricketts's most powerful words as well. Proofreaders of both type-script and the galleys wrote marginal notes suggesting that Steinbeck use another word. "Keep this word," he wrote in the margins. "There is no other English word like it." The word appears again in chapter 14. The idea is played out in the final scene.

From the random interaction of seed, turtle, human and animal movement, cars and trucks and soil—an assemblage of life—a new ecosystem emerges. Like the "survival symbol" at the novel's conclusion, like the grapes growing heavy for the vintage, like the small step forward, this chapter is parabolic, a snapshot of what emergence means. Just as Rose of Sharon's gesture brings some kind of sustenance to the old man, so may the seeds sprout and bring new life, so may the grapes be harvested. All are about life taking hold, reaching fruition.

CHAPTER 22

RICKETTS ON GRAPES

◆ ◆ ◆

IN MONTEREY, THERE was once a mural along Cannery Row, and on one panel Ed Ricketts's head floated above the canneries, like a god. He's viewed that way in the community where he lived, a guru and the nucleus of the lab group that attracted students from Stanford University's Hopkins Marine Station, visiting scientists, artists and writers, friends, two Jungian therapists, as well as Henry Miller and Krishnamurti and Burgess Meredith and Joseph Campbell and Charlie Chaplin—and of course John and Carol Steinbeck. This expansive, loose-jointed West Coast salon seemed to grow out of the pilings of the deck extending over the Pacific, like a barnacle or a clinging anemone, so much a part of the scene it was and is. The weathered lab still stands, and legendary Doc of *Cannery Row* and prophetic ecologist Ed Ricketts still inspire.

But Ricketts was also a tough-minded scientist—cool, dispassionate, rational. What follows are the two responses I know of that Ed made to *The Grapes of Wrath*.

When he heard Steinbeck read part of the book aloud (as was Steinbeck's habit) in June 1938, Ricketts wrote to a friend that

> [t]he new book will be utterly fine. Different form. No more fantasy. When he reads it I am tearful; realism with the deepest poetry of beauty. Jon seems to have gone some way in accepting the hazards and values of an enlarged horizon of consciousness.

And here is his later, more fully considered response:

> The "answer" to the "loving kindness" and the "all that lives is holy" thesis of *The Grapes of Wrath*, and to the "our loving kindness" and his "begats" idea is implicit in the words themselves: "all that lives is holy" applies to the other side as well, applies to the Farmers' Asso[ciation]. Jon says "have to fight," I say "ok" but realize the other side is in a "have to fight" also—and let your tenderness for the starving children of the one side apply to the children of the other side also even before they are killed, deprived of their homes or shocked; the other side "has to" fight also.
>
> "These evils are essential"; the struggle is nec-

essary. The struggle <u>is</u>; therefore the struggle is "<u>good</u>." And the children of the enemy are good. There isn't enough for everybody, therefore most people must go down in the struggle, either to the flat plane of mediocrity in a psychic sense . . . or to a physical death by starvation or being eaten up, and that's "good" too. People do the best they can and if they have to kill others to live, why they have to. "These evils are essential" so long, I suppose, as they have to, and these are varying in intensities of have to.

When he wrote *The Grapes of Wrath*, Steinbeck was a partisan, champion of the people, troubadour of change. Ricketts, on the other hand, was a detached observer. In Ricketts's response to *Grapes* is an explanation of what he called nonteleological thinking, an idea that intrigued and inspired Steinbeck as well: step back and observe what is, dispassionately and clearly. Do not focus on an end point—the teleology or result of a certain action. Do not focus on cause and effect or on a single explanation for complex situations. See the whole picture and accept, not with "supine and non-active acceptance of whatever is dished up," said Ricketts, but with full understanding and participation of what is: "The most active participation is involved with results in creative expression of some sort, possibly 'becoming,'" Ricketts explained.

For Ricketts, that broad acceptance of what *is* acknowledges and respects the fact that the Associated Farmers have emergent properties as well.

Ricketts wrote a similar response to the film Steinbeck worked on after *The Grapes of Wrath*—*The Forgotten Village*, a documentary about a cholera epidemic in a small Mexican village. In that film, Steinbeck champions modern medicine as a cure for village children with cholera. For Ricketts, bringing doctors and modern health care to the remote village destroys the community's faith in the *curandera*, their shaman and healer.

Ricketts's fervent belief in "breaking through" to the shimmering whole and his interest in emergent properties apparently did not apply to social solutions, to partisan fervor. Steinbeck's did—at least in 1939.

CHAPTER 23

THE BOOK

❖ ❖ ❖

STEINBECK'S EDITOR AND loyal friend Pat Covici wrote this to the author at a particularly difficult time in his life, when Steinbeck's second marriage was crumbling: "I should be with you today on your birthday because I shall always be glad that you were born and if I should leave before you, which is reasonable, I shall convince St. Peter to give me a handpress to work with and when you come you will write the little stories you always wanted to and I shall handprint them and distribute them and thus corrupt Heaven. Love Pat."

Covici believed fervently that a book was a beautiful object. Before he met Steinbeck in 1934, he had published many lavish volumes under the Covici-Friede imprint, special editions and risqué books like Radclyffe Hall's lesbian novel *The Well of Loneliness* (1928), a book he went to court to defend against censors. Covici was a Romanian pirate, chortled Arthur Miller (Covici was Miller's editor as well)—a cheerful, dapper, and determined old pirate, a kind and patient editor. He discovered copies of Steinbeck's early novels in a Chicago bookstore and, after he developed "a rather frantic regard for my work," said Steinbeck, he was signed on as editor in 1934.

Steinbeck's first novel that Covici published was *Tortilla Flat* in 1935, illustrated by Ruth Gannett, whose husband was the book critic with the *New York Herald Tribune*. In 1936 Covici issued *In Dubious Battle* in a trade copy as well as a limited edition of ninety-nine manually numbered copies, each with glassine cover and paperboard case, each signed by Steinbeck. The cost was a steep $5. (Today a pristine copy might fetch $12,000.) That Christmas, as a gift to clients, he printed 199 copies of Steinbeck's rollicking short story about a wicked, canonized pig, the satiric "Saint Katy the Virgin." The twenty-five-page volume was bound with a festive red and gold print cover and a golden spine, each book signed by the author. (It's a tough book to find if you're a collector, selling for upward of $3,000, more if it includes the Christmas greeting bookmark. If editor and writer could be here now, Covici would be delighted, Steinbeck chagrined. John once told a friend that he wouldn't spend $10 on a Gutenberg Bible. He didn't have the book collecting gene: "I simply don't understand it.")

The next year, Covici outdid himself for Steinbeck. In 1937, Covici-Friede published 2,500 copies of *Of Mice and Men* (no limited editions), and a limited edition of *The Red Pony*—699 numbered copies of three of the stories, all of which had been published separately in magazines. On the tan cover was stamped a rearing red pony and a slipcase was included. Steinbeck signed all 699 copies, accepting the fact that loyal Pat loved to issue expensive books with filigree descriptions: "set in monotype Italian Oldstyle and printed on hand-made La Garde paper." Since John and Carol went to New York City in the summer of 1937, Covici probably sat him down one afternoon in a sweltering New York City office with a pen and a pile of books. I know of no letter where Steinbeck complained about this task, although he did groan about the price, ten dollars. A decade later, Covici wanted to publish *The Pearl* in "one of your little literary jewel cases," as Steinbeck quipped. "I've always felt that they were kind of a gyp, but then you say no one forces any one to buy them." True enough.

By 1938, Covici-Friede's lavish ways, coupled with a sluggish economy, doomed the company. Pat couldn't pay Steinbeck $2,000 in royalties, and John fussed about Pat's creditors as he wrote the early chapters of *The Grapes of Wrath*: "Pat's trouble piddles on and that interferes some," Steinbeck wrote in the diary. "Don't know who will publish my book." Certainly it was not a happy situation for a stressed author, midbook. Other publishers came courting. Bennett Cerf from Random House met Steinbeck in San Francisco, introducing him for the first time to poet Robinson Jeffers, Steinbeck's Carmel neighbor. Scrappy Pat, however, landed a job as editor at Viking and brought Steinbeck with him. *The Long Valley*, a collection of short stories, was the first Steinbeck book the firm published in September 1938. *The Grapes of Wrath* was the second.

It's no wonder that Covici was thrilled about this epic written by "his" author.

But Steinbeck warned his ebullient editor not to print too many copies, because he was certain that *The Grapes of Wrath* would not be a popular book. Neither Covici nor Viking Press editors agreed, however, and Pat wrote John two months before publication asking if he could borrow the *Grapes* manuscript to display in Brentano's bookshop window: "This sort of thing has been done before I know, but yours is such an unusual manuscript and its display . . . would cause a great deal of exciting comment and most dignified publicity." John said no. The manuscript belonged to Carol, he wrote back to Pat, and furthermore, "what went into the writing of it is no business of the reader. I disapprove of having my crabbed hand exposed. The fact that my writing is small may be a marvel but it is completely unimportant to the book. . . . Let's have no personality at all."

John wanted this novel to stand on its own. He feared what might happen to his writing if a cult of personality encrusted him. Covici bowed to John's wishes, of course. But one can imagine his disappointment in not having the oversized ledger book, filled with Steinbeck's very small handwriting, on display at Brentano's, open, perhaps, to the first page, "New Start Big Writing." (This splendid document now resides in Special Collections at the University of Virginia.)

Steinbeck had reason enough to pull back. Publicity for the book was swelling. Viking's editorial and sales staffs were confident in a best seller and had allotted

$10,000 for the publicity campaign. Up to the date of publication, April 14, 1939, 45,918 books were shipped to sellers, confirming the company's faith in its popularity. Delighted with these numbers, the company added another $10,000 to the campaign budget. On June 6, Covici sent John a telegram: "We passed one hundred thousand mark with Grapes. Love Pat." Admitting that they "never had a book the sales rate of which approached this," Viking launched a "guessing contest on Steinbeck shipments"—how many books would Viking ship by December 31, 1939? "Send a postcard," readers were urged. Win twenty-five dollars.

The Grapes of Wrath topped best-seller lists in 1939. Readers devoured it. Critics lauded and lambasted it. Everyone in America, it seemed, knew about it. And *The Grapes of Wrath* was nudged along by a series of new ad campaigns: "between the end of July and the first of October an additional $40,000 will be spent on advertising *The Grapes of Wrath*," Pat wrote John. Christmas ads were bold and plain because, as the advertising firm told the Viking sales office, "the book was so famous that what was required was mainly a poster effect." The ad campaign handled the book "with great dignity as a literary masterpiece."

"Give the book everybody wants, the most famous . . . most praised . . . most popular novel of our time."

"Have you read the most famous book of our time?"

"Straight to the heart of every American," read a *Time* magazine ad.

"Into its second quarter-million," read a *New York Times* ad.

It sold steadily throughout 1939, about 3,000–4,000 copies a week.

By the fall of 1939, noted a reporter for *Publishers Weekly*, the novel "had figured in so many news stories and editorials that the press of the country was using the words 'Joad' and 'Okie' without explaining them." While it took a bit longer, even staunchly conservative *Reader's Digest* published an excerpt in the fall of 1940, "Two for a Penny," chapter 15 of the novel. The magazine omitted the waitress Mae's offending line: " 'Truck drivers,' Mae said reverently, 'an' after them shitheels.' " More significantly, perhaps, they chose the chapter that is a sanitized message of the whole—care about one family and problems are resolved. The book insists, however, that tough issues— land use, indifference of the used-car salesmen, violence of the Associated Farmers—aren't solved with a smile.

By the end of 1939, 430,000 books had sold. Someone won twenty-five dollars. (It was a good year for counting things, as this frothy and emblematic story conveys— escape from Depression woe was an attractive option. The month before *The Grapes of Wrath* was published, a Harvard undergraduate swallowed a live goldfish. The college campus goldfish-swallowing craze was on. At Franklin and Marshall, an undergrad salted, peppered, and swallowed three the following week. Back to Harvard, where twenty-four were ingested by a woozy student. Then to Penn, twenty-five, followed by a steak dinner to calm a churning stomach. The champion goldfish swallower for that year was Joseph Deliberto, who attended Clark University.)

Grapes won a Pulitzer Prize in 1940.

It won the National Book Award with a unanimous vote. At their February 17 luncheon at New York City's Hotel Astor, the National Book Award committee announced that *Grapes* was the "Booksellers' Favorite Novel" and *Johnny Got His Gun* by Dalton Trumbo was "The Most Original Book of the Year." To honor its five-hundredth anniversary that year, a copy of the Gutenberg Bible was on display, loaned by the General Theological Seminary.

If you had purchased one of the first 45,918 copies of *The Grapes of Wrath* in 1939—the first edition—you knew it because "First Edition" was stamped in bold on the inside fold of the dust jacket, lower right corner. On page 270, line 2, there was a typo, "What you go there," not recognized until years later, in the corrected Library of America edition edited by Robert DeMott. In the first edition, the dedication to Steinbeck's wife, Carol, reads "To Carol who willed it," corrected later that year to "To Carol who willed this book." In 1939, all copies sold for $2.75.

Today, with the original dust jacket and in pristine condition, this book sells for $10,000 or sometimes much more. If inscribed to a person or signed by Steinbeck, a great deal more. A friend of mine, who collects twentieth-century first editions, has looked for a signed, uninscribed copy of *The Grapes of Wrath* for over thirty years. Every copy he has seen advertised has been inscribed to someone. I don't have a copy myself, signed or not, although I try to help my friend locate the signed book he believes is out there somewhere. And while I'm in Steinbeck's camp regarding book collecting, there are few exceptional volumes on my shelves, and one is a worn and cherished *Grapes*, which I prefer to a pristine first. Many years ago, a woman who knew Steinbeck in the 1930s, Margaret Ringnalda, gave me her copy, the tenth printing of 1939, worn at the corners, she said, because it was passed around to everyone she knew. It's my legacy book, much beloved, touched by hands that helped the migrants.

Carol Steinbeck's dedication copy of *Grapes* was bound in leather. In May, Steinbeck requested fifteen more copies bound in "either leather or a distinctive cloth" with a leaf tipped in "indicating a special edition of 15." Pat wrote back to say that the books would cost twelve to fifteen dollars a copy if they were bound "in the same way as Carol's copy," but he could bind them in cheap leather for less. Steinbeck, I believe, chose fifteen copies of the expensive leather and donated the books to a "tremendous banquet in Hollywood to raise money for the migrants." Earlier in the year, he had lent his name to the John Steinbeck Committee, organized by Helen Gahagan Douglas for migrant relief, a cause he passionately endorsed. It took me years to see one of these books, which I hardly believed existed. Helen Gahagan Douglas's copy, like the others, has a page inserted: "At the request of John Steinbeck fifteen numbered and signed copies of this book were especially bound for the Steinbeck Migrant Organization (May 25, 1939)." Now that's a book I would like to own.

Covici wrote Steinbeck in August 1939, suggesting another limited edition of the novel. He wanted 3,000 copies, "printed on rag paper, numbered and signed for the Fall of 1940" (more books for Steinbeck to sign!) and "illustrated by some American artist. Have you any preferences? How would you like it if we announced an award for $1,000 or $1,500 to the artist who submits the most satisfying drawings for the book?"

As it turned out, Thomas Hart Benton, an illustrator for the Limited Editions Club, was assigned the book, a two-volume boxed set, published in 1940. It was an "inevitable" choice, art critic Thomas Craven writes in his introduction to the volume; "this alliance between artist and author is one of the happiest and wisest that has been effected in the annals of American illustration." Benton was born in Neosho, Missouri, about forty miles from Sallisaw, Oklahoma, and shared Steinbeck's social vision—he was "fundamentally a social radical," said his biographer. In the late 1920s, as restless as was Steinbeck himself, Benton had walked across the United States, sketching steel mills, lumber camps, coal mines, and cotton fields—and then integrated those sketches of working Americans into *America Today* (1930), a mural that he painted for the New School for Social Research in New York City. The commission made him famous, and he would paint several other murals in the next few years.

In 1932, he illustrated a Marxist history of the United States, *We, the People*, also drawing from his travel sketches. Hired as an illustrator when the Limited Editions Club was launched in 1938, Benton's first project was *Tom Sawyer*; his second, *The Grapes of Wrath*, for which he produced sixty-one two-color lithographs, yellow and black. While the drawings are clear and unsentimental—some based on another sketching trip he took to Independence, Missouri, in April 1940, others based on images from the film—they lack the political snap of his earlier sketches.

In 1964, Steinbeck sent this to Thomas Hart Benton: "I salute your distinguished career with special enthusiasm because of what it has meant to me personally in friendship and in my work. Your sympathetic illustrations for *The Grapes of Wrath* added a visual dimension to my novel and left me in your debt."

"This year has been a wonderful one for us," Covici wrote to Steinbeck in December 1939, "due largely to you. Quite aside from the good business *The Grapes of Wrath* has meant, it has given us all the greatest satisfaction to be associated with it."

And he wrote on October 9, 1940, to say that four new editions of *Grapes* would be out. "The book still marches on."

It marched to World War II in a 1943 Armed Services edition, part of a series of pocketbooks printed for soldiers because books were "one of the weapons in the war of ideas." Books "sustain morale." Distributed free to servicemen overseas, the little volumes were meant for a breast pocket, meant to be passed on to other soldiers. No copies were sold or remaindered. (About fifty copies a month were selected during the war, seven titles by Steinbeck. That was more than his male modernist contemporaries—two by Faulkner, two by Hemingway, and three by Fitzgerald.)

And it marched on through the twentieth century, never out of print, selling over 100,000 copies a year (1980s) and 150,000 a year in the 1990s. In 1989, when Viking published *Working Days: Steinbeck's Journal of "The Grapes of Wrath,"* to coincide with the fiftieth anniversary, 14,000 were printed and sold out before the April 14 release. And 25,000 new hard copy editions of the novel with an introduction by Studs Terkel sold out by May.

And it marches on into the twenty-first century, translated into at least forty-five languages, including Sorani Kurdish, Serbo-Croatian, Macedonian, Belarusian, Albanian, Vietnamese, and Marathi.

The most expensive copy of *The Grapes of Wrath* that I know to have sold went for $47,800 at auction in 2007, a copy inscribed to Steinbeck's sister Beth. The auction house claimed that it was a "world record for an at-auction" Steinbeck novel. And I'm sure that's right.

Pat Covici must be in a book heaven, with his letter-press, smiling broadly. When he died in 1964, Steinbeck wrote this about his editor of nearly thirty years:

> Pat Covici was much more than my friend. He was my editor. Only a writer can understand how a great editor is father, mother, teacher, personal devil and personal god. For thirty years Pat was my collaborator and my conscience. He demanded of me more than I had and thereby caused me to be more than I should have been without him.

CHAPTER 24

REACTIONS

◆ ◆ ◆

IN THE LOCAL section of the August 24, 1939, edition of the *Bakersfield Californian*, a picture of book burning ran under the header "Farmers Burn 'Grapes.'" Actually the picture shows two farmers, one the president of the Kern County Associated Farmers, flanking one migrant who is tossing *The Grapes of Wrath* into a flaming waste can. It was a disturbing image that showed clearly, as journalist Frank J. Taylor wrote in *Forum* that November, that "Californians are wrathy over *The Grapes of Wrath*. Though the book is fiction, many readers accept it as fact."

Literal and figurative fires ignited after the April 14 publication of *The Grapes of Wrath*. While the majority of thoughtful and positive reviews probably equaled if not outweighed the vituperative attacks, accusations are always far juicier than plaudits. Logs were piled on the conflagration by pundits, by the Associated Farmers, and by a very wrathy Oklahoma congressman, Lyle Boren, who stood up in Congress and said that *Grapes* was a "lie, a black infernal creation of a twisted, distorted mind."

With only ten pages written, Steinbeck had despaired of what was in store for him with a book that pulled no punches: "The Greeks seem to have known about this dark relationship between luck and destruction," he wrote in his journal. The words were prophetic. When *Grapes* soared to the top of the best-seller lists, it nearly destroyed the author, emotionally, physically, artistically. Fame, something he had always feared, claimed his soul. To him, *Grapes* seemed a Faustian pact. "Now I have what is called success," he wrote to his uncle Joe Hamilton. "Every liberal organization in the country is living my life for me, plotting my work for me, telling me how to think, how to work, what to do; telling me who my enemies are and my friends, defining my politics and my sympathies, typing me, making a symbol of me, in fact, on a vastly larger and more clever scale, doing just what mother did when she insisted that I be a lawyer and an Episcopalian."

Steinbeck's name slapped on an ad demonstrated engagement: in April 1940, a forthcoming forum in *Theatre Arts* magazine was announced with the headline "Calling John Steinbeck," noting that conditions on Broadway were "almost as tough" as on California farms, with only twenty-two legitimate productions, thousands of actors out of work, and young people unable to get a start.

The Steinbeck name had become an imprimatur of social action.

Both John and Carol Steinbeck were overwhelmed by the money and the letters that poured in as well as the protests and the fame. The woman who had "willed" the book into being—as the dedication notes—the woman who had a social conscience initially more muscular than her husband's, the woman who had believed in his writing for eleven years, the woman who typed every manuscript, who gave titles to *Of Mice and Men* and *The Grapes of Wrath*, who had helped with the organization of several books and brought him stories for some and edited every one, the woman who was his muse and mainstay, his wife and his soul mate—that woman seemed alien. John would get involved with another woman who was sexy and playful (one can't help but think of her as an antidote to migrant problems) and separated from Carol two years after the book's publication. The Steinbecks were leveled by *Grapes*.

Probably no book published in the twentieth century created the firestorm that *The Grapes of Wrath* set off. "'Grapes of Wrath'? Obscenity and Inaccuracy" read an *Oklahoma City Times* headline on May 4, 1939. That set out the two lines of attack. In Buffalo, New York, "vulgar words" stopped the librarian from purchasing copies, it was reported. Kansas City, Missouri, librarians objected to the indecent portrayal of women and for "portray[ing] life in such a bestial way." The head librarian at the San Jose public library, about ten miles from Steinbeck's home, banned the book as "unfit for its patrons. Applicants are told it can be had at the circulating book stores." The library did not carry a single volume of Steinbeck's work in 1939: "a line must be drawn somewhere" sniffed the librarian. Of course, like all book banning, that just made the novel more scintillating.

Another attacking flank zeroed in on the book's political stance and "inaccuracies." In California, Pro-America, a women's group with ties to the Associated Farmers, accused Steinbeck of fomenting class hatred. The Associated Farmers "have tried to make me retract things by very sly methods. Unfortunately for them, the things are thoroughly documented and the materials turned over to the La Follette Committee," Steinbeck wrote to his college roommate. The Associated Farmers were out to get him. Hearst papers went for him. One article is sufficiently overwrought to represent the most vitriolic: "The Truth About California," screamed an oversized headline in the *San Francisco Examiner* on January 14, 1940, beneath which ran "Red Ousters Urged as State's Only Solution to End Migrant Evil," the second of a two-part series by Elsie Robinson, once a migrant laborer, who took on the task of refuting the "slurs cast upon California" by "Comrade Steinbeck." Farmhands received the highest wages of any state, save Connecticut, said Elsie, with a base rate of $2.10 with board, a "square deal." But then the migrants came "with their urgent need and inferior traditions" and underbid the "regular workers." In her eyes, farmers were merely "frightened citizens" who deserved our pity. California's tax rolls were strained by the "migrant menace," she continued, and oldsters threatened to get more. "THE JOADS ARE SETTLING DOWN—ENJOYING HEALTH AND COMFORT THEY'VE NEVER KNOWN BEFORE." (The photo depicts a family with

nine children—accepting California's gifts.) She contin-
ued: Watch out California! And even worse, most won't
settle down because they came here not out of need, but
because they were restless, "shiftless white trash." "BUT
A 100 PER CENT AMERICAN HAS AN ITCHING
HEEL, AS WELL AS ANY ALIEN TRAMP. . . . THE
WHOLE DESIGN OF MODERN LIFE HAS STIMU-
LATED THEIR HUNGER FOR CHANGE AND AD-
VENTURE, FUN AND FRIPPERY. GIVE THEM A
RELIEF CHECK AND THEY'LL HEAD STRAIGHT
FOR A BEAUTY SHOP AND A MOVIE."

Several Californians got busy with more creative responses. *Plums of Plenty*, a three-reel film written and
directed by the secretary of the Kern County Chamber
of Commerce, was shown at the San Francisco Golden
Gate International Exposition in 1939. (Emory G. Hoff-
man defended his film, which depicted the generosity toward migrants in Kern County: "The torch of civilization
burns a little brighter, a little higher, in Kern County
than in the rest of the world.") *Grapes of Gladness* was a
novel written by a Los Angeles real estate developer who
chided migrants for turning north rather than south toward Los Angeles, where they could have bought a small
lot and become self-sufficient gardeners in a Thoreauvean
mold—*Walden* was quoted on the cover. And Steinbeck's
Los Gatos neighbor Ruth Comfort Mitchell wrote *Of
Human Kindness*, a romance about small farmers (to
prove that California had them): an Okie wanders onto
tidy acres, is cleaned up, taught to speak properly, and
marries the farmer's daughter.

Rick Wartzman has written a lengthy account of the

Bakersfield Board of Supervisors' vote to ban *The Grapes of Wrath* in Kern County. One voice in that flap stands out in my mind. At a meeting held in response to the supervisors' ban, a black man stood up and said that "*Uncle Tom's Cabin* had done much for the abolition of slavery and that *The Grapes of Wrath* sought to abolish 'economic' slavery in California." He concluded his comments: "Today they tell us that the migrants are nice, God-fearing, moral people. A year ago," he continued, holding up newspaper articles that quoted local members of the Associated Farmers, "they told us in their publications that the migrants were dirty, immoral scum, who lived under crowded, immoral conditions and lay naked in the fields."

That seems a courageous voice at that moment, in that place.

Steinbeck took note of the controversy, writing a letter of thanks to the lone supervisor who had voted against the Bakersfield ban, almost the only time he got involved in any of the publicity: "I have not felt it necessary to defend myself against the Associated Farmers or the Pro-America group. Their stupidity in applying the vigilante methods of their labor relations to literary criticism was immediately obvious to the people of California for whom they presume to speak."

For years after, Oklahomans bristled at the name Steinbeck, an author who had "all but destroyed the morale of Oklahomans," noted University of Oklahoma regents, and made them feel "apologetic" about living in the state. In 1945, the regents came up with an antidote: a powerhouse football team. A year later, Governor Robert Kerr thought that the musical *Oklahoma!* would help erase the damage Steinbeck had done and hosted a lavish welcome to a 1946 touring show and made Rodgers and Hammerstein honorary Kiowa Indians. For the state's fiftieth anniversary, the Semi-Centennial Committee invited Steinbeck to the state—causing a firestorm of protest. The image of an ignorant Okie rankled.

Timing is everything. Had *Grapes* been published a year or two later, it would have been swamped by preparation for World War II—even in 1939, attention was shifting from the home front to the crisis in Europe, what Steinbeck called the "troubled world soul." Oklahoman Sanora Babb, the woman featured in Ken Burns's film about the Dust Bowl, submitted four chapters of her novel on Southwest migrants to Bennett Cerf at Random House three months after *The Grapes of Wrath* was published. *Grapes* had already commanded the attention of a nation.

CHAPTER 25

Did *The Grapes of Wrath* Help the Migrants?

♦ ♦ ♦

SHORTLY BEFORE HE completed the novel, John Steinbeck agreed to be state chairman of the Committee to Aid Agricultural Organization, which met in Bakersfield, California, on October 28, 1938, attracting an audience of 350. Although he was not in attendance, he would have approved the letter the committee sent to the Farm Security Administration in Washington, D.C.: "The 9 Farm Security Administration camps now operating accommodate 200 families, a small fraction of the 25,000 estimated to be totally without housing, living on ditch banks with no safe source of drinking water and no facilities for garbage and sewage disposal." And the average yearly wage for a migrant worker in California was $450. The minimum cost for an adequate diet for a family of four, according to the Department of Agriculture, was $475.

The Steinbeck Committee sent a telegram to President Roosevelt in February 1939 protesting cuts to the FSA and camp program and another telegram "for the continuation and extension of the La Follette Civil Liberties Committee." That finally happened. In 1936, a Senate committee had been formed to investigate labor unions and management disputes around the country. Chaired by Robert Marion La Follette Jr. of Wisconsin, the committee that bore his name held preliminary investigations of conditions in California in 1936 and 1938. In December 1939, with additional funding and increased pressure to investigate labor/management problems, the La Follette Committee held hearings in Los Angeles and San Francisco. The final report, notes California historian Kevin Starr, is "an assemblage of narrative, testimony, excerpted statement, and documentary evidence that speaks with one vast collective voice . . . [it] represents history as the search for moral meaning." And the La Follette report corroborated everything that Steinbeck wrote in *The Grapes of Wrath*: "The essential thesis of *Violations of Free Speech and Rights of Labor*," Starr asserts, "is nothing less than the existence in California in the 1930s of a conspiracy to suppress constitutional rights that, in a comparison made frequently in the report, made California seem more a fascist European dictatorship than part of the United States."

Steinbeck had not lied. "I've seen some of the private reports to the La Follette Committee," he wrote to his college roommate in January 1940. "It is amazing how readily some of our best citizens will take up murder. It would be healthy I think if a few could be hanged. You should hear some of the threats made against me. They are melodramatic. The best was from a man who said I would never get out of this world alive. Be a good trick if I could."

But it was hardly a jocular matter, as Steinbeck knew. Neither the publication of *The Grapes of Wrath*, nor the formation of the John Steinbeck Committee, nor the findings of the La Follette Committee changed wages substantially, or caused more government camps to be built, or eased labor/management tensions.

But the documentary outrage of the late 1930s had a lasting impact, if not immediately political then broadly cultural. What *The Grapes of Wrath* achieved was represented most visibly by Eleanor Roosevelt's compassion. When she toured camps in 1940 to survey the situation described in *The Grapes of Wrath*, she went to a government camp at Visalia and then an Oildale Hooverville "where she picked up a child who had impetigo and rebuked the camp manager for allowing a water faucet to be attached to a privy."

Attitudes shift ever so slowly. *The Grapes of Wrath* probably had its greatest impact on a personal level, shifting sensibilities, touching hearts. And Steinbeck's mournful book was and is read around the world. In Russia it was translated immediately and published in 1940. In China as well.

I have this scrap in a file that Steinbeck biographer

Jackson Benson gave me—a John Steinbeck quote, with no source:

> People . . . automatically believe in books. This is strange but it is so. Messages come from behind the controlled and censored areas of the world and they do not ask for radios, for papers and pamphlets. They invariably ask for books. They believe books when they believe nothing else.

CHAPTER 26

THE FILM

◆ ◆ ◆

IN 1966, STEINBECK sat down to watch John Ford's film of *The Grapes of Wrath*, twenty-six years after its January 1940 release. "Times pass; we change; the urgency departs," he noted about his reluctance to watch the movie again. But "then a lean, stringy, dark-faced piece of electricity walked out on the screen, and he had me. I believed my own story again. It was fresh and happening and good." What a tribute, spot-on. Henry Fonda as Tom Joad, the loner come home, brings viewers to the wasteland of Oklahoma, to Ma, and to empathy for working folks.

Ford's is a powerful, visually arresting film—not Steinbeck's novel, to be sure, but a sturdy and compelling work in its own right, a rendering of migrant woe pitched to a mass audience. After producer Darryl F. Zanuck purchased the rights to the book for $75,000, Steinbeck insisted that Tom Collins be hired as a technical director:

he wanted no lies, no blurring of conditions. He added a clause to the contract: "The producer agrees that any motion picture based on the said literary property shall fairly and reasonably retain the main action and social intent of said literary property." But Steinbeck also recognized that any writer, any director, creates a separate vision from the writer's. He told screenwriter Nunnally Johnson, "You can make a good picture out of [it] and I hope you do, but my statement remains right there, in the book, that's all." Johnson agreed with that stance: "A screenwriter's duty, his loyalty, is not to the book. Whenever I work on these things, my eye is on the audience, not on the author." Johnson's intention was simply to show "the plight of some very ordinary people." And to end with "some ray of hope—something that would keep the people who saw it from going out and getting so drunk in utter despondency that they couldn't tell other people that it was a good picture to see." That's precisely what the film accomplishes with the final cut, apparently determined by Darryl Zanuck: Ma's speech about the people going on.

Without a doubt, Ford's movie softens the book's message. As several critics have noted, the explanatory scroll at the beginning of the film locates the material safely in the past (and "Red River Valley," played over and over in the film, heightens the nostalgic tone). The film omits much of the material in the interchapters— thus blurring the economic and historical punch of the text as well as its mythical layer. Jane Darwell as Ma Joad is probably too old for the part—Steinbeck thought so— making Ma squishier and more sentimental than Steinbeck's Ma (Darwell won the Academy Award for the part, however). The authenticity that Ford cultivated feels a little too folksy, as reported in the press book for the film. In those pages one learns that Henry Fonda went to Oklahoma to mingle with migrants. And John Carradine, who plays a gaunt, haunted Casy, lived his part as a bedraggled migrant—his car broke down on the way to the studio one day, and the Los Angeles police picked him up for vagrancy as he hitchhiked to work. The studio worked hard to locate the film firmly in a not-too-harsh contemporary world.

"It isn't elaborate realism that counts," Ford insisted, "but the plain, homey touches for which a director must try"—Ma sadly burning her letters, alone in the dark. The press book counseled theater owners to emphasize the human angle, perhaps sponsor a Ma Joad writing contest: "Every woman can appreciate the great human problem that faced Ma Joad. For the best 200 word letters on this subject: 'How can a mother help keep a family together in the face of all adversity?' [Newspaper] is offering the following prizes [List cash prizes and number of guest tickets here]." The film's emphasis on heartwarming strength of purpose isn't far from what Steinbeck was after in the novel, but the film nudges closer to what the book sidesteps—overt sentimentality.

Promotional posters, visuals, and articles all taught audiences to concentrate on surfaces and characters. John Ford commissioned a series of five lithographs from Thomas Hart Benton—portraits of Ma, Tom, Rose of Sharon, Casy, and Pa—and these heads mediate between the subject matter, poverty, and a mass audience wary of poverty. Portraiture focuses attention on faces of woe, not a systemic failure of capitalism, and years later, Ford admitted as much. He was "only interested in the Joad family as characters. . . . I was not interested in *Grapes* as a social study."

Gregg Toland's cinematography preserves the visual intensity of the book—something Steinbeck appreciated the first time he saw the film, a "hard straight picture . . . that looks and feels like a documentary film and . . . has a hard, truthful ring," he said on December 15, 1939, after seeing the preview.

In January 1940, when the film premiered in New York City (the Associated Farmers rumbled about trouble with a California opening), Steinbeck was a "household name," as advertising insisted, and *Grapes* was still on best-seller lists. The film was a blockbuster, angering some, pleasing others. My favorite review, I think, is Woody Guthrie's, who commented on the film in "Woody Sez," his column for the West Coast Communist Party newspaper, *People's World*.

Seen the pitcher last night, "Grapes of Wrath," best cussed pitcher I ever seen . . . about us a pullin' out of Oklahoma and Arkansas, and down south and out, and a driftin' around over the State of California, busted, disgusted, down and out, and a lookin' for work.

. . . It says you got to get together and have some meetins, and stick together and raise old billy hell till you get your job, and get your farm back, and your house and your chickens, and your groceries and your clothes, and your money back.

Go to see "Grapes of Wrath" pardner, go to see it and don't miss. You was the star in that picture. Go and see your own self, and hear your own words and your own songs.

That's good advice. Think about your own self as you hear Tom Joad/Henry Fonda speak those words.

CHAPTER 27

"NONE OF IT IS IMPORTANT OR ALL OF IT IS."

◆ ◆ ◆

CHAPTERS 22–26, IN which the Joads find a temporary home at the government camp, rise to a great crescendo. They are the book's emergent center. The chapters move from particular to general, from notes of sadness to the thunder of action—from the tide pool to the stars, in fact. All of it is important or none of it is.

The end of chapter 22 is another piece of coral—a bittersweet and lovely little scene. The Joads are newly ensconced in the government camp, which will be their home for a month. Finally clean and safe after their long journey, Ma, her head in her hand, sits mournfully in front of their tent—another threshold—and sad memories come "a-flockin' back": Granma's burial and Noah's and Connie's desertion. And she remembers the chopping block at home. Squatting before her, Pa "took on her tone" as he describes a wedge of ducks he saw that day, and blackbirds on wires and doves on fences, his refrain twice voiced. Ma responds, "Remember what we'd always say at home? 'Winter's a-comin' early' we said, when the ducks flew." Her flock of thoughts becomes his of birds, and their mingled nostalgic voices and vision bring solace, not melancholia. The wedge of ducks gives Ma a healing thought: "They's things you do, an' you don' know why"—just like ducks flying in a wedge, just like migrants trudging on. This duet frees Ma to voice the book's melody—we're the people and we survive.

Once known as "immigrant psychosis," nostalgia is instead healing, as recent studies have shown, and deeply human. Ma perks up and, renewed, chides Pa for continuing to feeling guilty about Noah's birth, and then she chides Uncle John for doubting that Tom will return to the Weedpatch camp: "They's stuff you're sure of," says stick-wielding Ma, back to her fierce self. Just as Tom returned home from jail at the opening of the novel, she knows he will again—and so honors that familial bond with something "nice" for dinner, just as she did in Oklahoma. The scene is intimate, therapeutic, hopeful—and familiar. It is another beginning for the Joads. It is, in fact, the Joads' story etched in miniature.

Interchapter 23 expands this trio of healing voices to a choir: "The migrant people, scuttling for work, scrabbling to live, looked always for pleasure. . . ." In stories they find joy, and in movies, where one migrant sees "my life, an' more'n my life, so everything is bigger." And migrants find relief in liquor, "and everything's holy—everything, even me." And in music. And maybe even in religion. All these pleasures and distractions scoop up one migrant into something larger.

That larger unit is muscular in chapter 24, when the migrant "wall of men" prevent the three intruders at the Weedpatch Saturday night dance from causing a fight—taking swift and effective action. (Steinbeck based this episode on historical record—Tom Collins's reports on the government camp at Arvin.) And in chapter 25, Steinbeck warns that migrant anger may explode into something much larger and more powerful—sounding the book's deepest melody: "In the souls of the people the grapes of wrath are filling and growing heavy, growing heavy for the vintage." Before the Joads leave Weedpatch, in chapter 26, there is talk of unions, and the potential for migrant power: "Jus' stick together. They ain't raisin' hell with no two hundred men. They're pickin' on one man."

All five layers are in these Weedpatch chapters, the apogee of this novel. Integrating layers leads to what Ricketts calls "true ecology in which the important thing is neither the region, or the association, or the animal itself . . . or its various stages or needs, or even the ecological niche, but in which the unit is the relationship." Integration was Ricketts's intent as an ecologist. It was Steinbeck's intent as a writer.

When this book turned fifty, the country took note. Steppenwolf Theater Company in Chicago took its stark adaptation to London and San Diego and New York, where the theater critic Frank Rich wrote that Steppenwolf "[m]akes Steinbeck live for a new generation not by updating his book but by digging into its timeless heart," a sentence I love. That year, I kept a file of articles about the novel's golden anniversary, and when I recently made a list of the headlines and key words, I had a poem of sorts. The lyrical punch of headlines and commentaries tells a story:

"Why Steinbeck's Okies Speak to Us Today"
"We still see their faces"
And *The Grapes of Wrath*
"still holds power" and
"still packs a punch" and
"lives on" with its
"myth and misery" a
"timeless tale." *The Grapes of Wrath* is
"still controversial and poignant" and it
"hasn't gone sour" but is
"still fresh on the vine,"
"At 50, *Grapes of Wrath* thrives on vine,"

because "he opened the eyes of the educated middle class to the terrible deprivation and pain being suffered by the migrants and helped create a climate of sympathy and concern for them" (Jonathan Yardley)

and because he suggested that "running like a river beneath the surface of the nation's cold, hard, individualistic culture lies the spirit of Ma Joad, a spirit of 'fambly' and community that, once tapped, might redeem us all" (Alan Brinkley)

and because, I would add, Steinbeck
suggests how we might attend to the world,
acknowledging interconnections that bind
the local to the political, the familial to the
communal, the broken piece of coral to
the bombs that fall.

To read or perhaps to reread *The Grapes of Wrath* in the twenty-first century is to follow the book's five layers down, from surface clarity (so very much like gazing into a tide pool) to associations, histories, and universal symbols—finally to "breaking through," in Ricketts's term, to some notion of becoming something finer, purer, more fully a part of the whole shebang. *The Grapes of Wrath* is not a book to be shelved with histories of the 1930s. In five ways, on five layers, it's an urgent book.

It is not a novel of social reform, not a book that poses solutions to the economic, ecological, and sociological challenges of the 1930s. It is not a novel advocating higher wages or better housing or kinder owners, although surely Steinbeck would have endorsed all of that. Instead, his message is a message to the human heart, capable of "thinking, feeling, intuition, sensation." Life is worth living for all, whether a turtle, a seed, the displaced migrants—or an old, old man. Steinbeck's deep admiration for the migrants was coupled with a belief in their role in some kind of change, whatever that might be: They "think clearly," he said as he was beginning to write the novel. "I've wondered about this clarity of thought and it occurs to me that, coming from an agrarian pattern and being suddenly confronted with our capitalist industrialism, the paradoxes and ridiculous thinking of that system is doubly apparent . . . these migrant people with their clear thrust are destined to be a large determining factor in the imminent social change. And I love them for it."

The word that is important here is imminent, a word that echoes emergence and anlage. Fifteen years later, Steinbeck noted this in a 1954 interview: "I hold that man is largely an optimist, a scraper of starlight and that this, in practical life, is what has made his life better."

Pat Covici thought the same. On November 17, 1938, even before Steinbeck had sent the complete manuscript of *The Grapes of Wrath* to Viking Press, kindly Pat wrote to buoy the writer's spirits: "I would like to be shown a more significant piece of fiction than 'Grapes of Wrath' written in America." That letter is hyperbolic—*Grapes* may not be the most significant book in twentieth-century America. But considering what we're up against— ever sharper divisions between haves and have-nots; ever more incendiary debates about immigration; ever more powerful and wealthy banks; an ever more imperiled physical world, global warming hardly a myth—it seems so. *The Grapes of Wrath* reminds us that the Joads' story is, in many ways, our own—if we consider the American experiment as communal, if we do not isolate our story from the dispossessed of the world, if we embrace an "enlarged horizon of consciousness."

NOTES

• ◆ •

CITED ARE SECONDARY works not clearly referenced in the text or included in the bibliography. Abbreviations are as follows: *"America and Americans" and Selected Nonfiction*, AA; *A Life in Letters*, LL; *Working Days: The Journals of "The Grapes of Wrath,"* WD. Steinbeck is JS and Ricketts is ER. Library collections are cited in full once, a brief reference thereafter. The Martha Heasley Cox Center for Steinbeck Studies at San Jose State University is CSS. Dates for JS letters often note only the year, since Steinbeck did not date many of his letters in the 1920s and 1930s.

PREFACE

x   **"outcasts in a hostile society"**: William Kennedy, "My Work Is No Good," *New York Times Book Review*, April 9, 1989, 1, 44.

CHAPTER I · NEW START BIG WRITING

2   **"draft with a pen, you know"**: JS to folks, 1927. Wells Fargo Collection, M1063, Department

of Special Collections, Stanford University
Libraries.

2   **"Very dear pen"**: Long Valley Ledger, CSS, San Jose
State University.

2   **"I gloat"**: JS to George and Anne Albee, January 9,
1937, George Sumner, Albee Papers, BANC MSS
C-H 120, Bancroft Library, University of California,
Berkeley.

2–3 **"pencils like butter . . . pencils"**: JS to Jules Buck,
April 15, 1950, John Steinbeck Collection, MO263,
Department of Special Collections, Stanford.

6   **"actually wrote"**: Thomas Fensch, *Conversations
with John Steinbeck* (Jackson: University Press of
Mississippi, 1988), 85.

6   **"'big writing does not'"**: "Wayward Bus"
Journal, Pierpont Morgan Library, Department
of Literary and Historical Manuscripts,
New York, NY.

6   **"The Original Manuscript"**: Roy Simmonds, *San
Jose Studies* 16 (1990): 117–32.

CHAPTER 2 · FIVE LAYERS

8   **"more than he has in himself"**: JS to Pascal Covici,
January 1939, Viking files.

9   **"no horizons"**: "About Ed Ricketts," *AA*, 188.

9   **"sparked one another"**: Frances Strong to
Joel Hedgpeth, May 3, 1970, Ed Ricketts Jr.
Collection, private collection.

9   **"four approaches"**: ER, in Rodger, ed., *Breaking
Through*, 259–61.

12 **"breaking through"**: ER, in Rodger, ed.,
Renaissance Man of Cannery Row, 52.

12   **"straight on something, is immanent"**: JS to Albee, 1934, Bancroft Library, Berkeley.

CHAPTER 3 · "STAY WITH THE DETAIL."

14   **marine educator:** Dr. Craig Strang is the associate director of Lawrence Hall of Science, University of California, Berkeley.

14   **Steinbeck Institute:** See "John Steinbeck, The Voice of a Region, a Voice for America, www .Steinbeckinstitute.org.

15   **"survival in the intertidal":** E-mail to author from Martin Zotolo.

15   **"moving kidney":** Dan Clare, "The Illustrious Sea Hare," video.

15   **"Stay with the detail":** *WD*, 39.

16   **"little snow drifts":** Long Valley Ledger, CSS.

18   **"grounded in this theme":** JS to Harry Guggenheim, February 15, 1966, copies at CSS.

18   **"deceptive simplicity":** Peter Matthiessen, in Susan Shillinglaw, ed., *Centennial Reflections by American Writers* (San Jose, CA: Center for Steinbeck Studies, 2002), 63.

19   **"it distracts me":** JS to Annie Laurie Williams, April 20, 1938, Rare Book and Manuscript Library, Butler Library, Columbia University.

20   **"know it with my ear":** JS to Covici, January 31, 1939, Viking files.

20   **"capable of anything":** JS to Mr. Criswell, n.d., author's files.

20   **"streetwise prose are with us still":** Kazin, *American Dreamers*, 143.

21   **"feeney bush":** JS to Joseph Henry Jackson, 1939.

JH Jackson Papers, BANC MSS C-H 40, Bancroft Library, Berkeley.

23   "**picture while I'm working**": *WD*, 29.

CHAPTER 4 · SCIENTIST AND WRITER

26   "**own ends . . . threaten the existence of the species**": JS to Joe Hamilton, October 23, 1939, Wells Fargo Collection, Stanford.

26   "**contradiction in terms**": Paul de Kreif to ER, 1939, Edward Flanders Ricketts Papers, MO219, Stanford.

26   "**stickler for factual truth**": ER, Post Fire Notebook III, Ed Ricketts Jr. Collection.

26–27 "**reason and of its possibilities**": ER, *Renaissance Man*, 146.

27   "**greatest book I've ever come in contact with**": ER, ibid., 267.

27   "**pioneering and much needed sort**": ER Papers, Box 11, Stanford.

28   "**of Whitman and Jeffers**": "A Spiritual Morphology of Poetry": ER, *Breaking Through*, 105–18.

28   "**wave shock**": ER Papers, Box 12, Stanford.

28   "**relation being significant**": ER, unpublished "Zoological Introduction" to "Between Pacific Tides," 1936, ER Papers, Stanford.

29   "**He was very observant**": Lillith James interview with author, March 1, 1988.

30   "**fine judgment of children**": JS to Ben Abramson, 1936, John Steinbeck Collection, TXRCOO-A9, Harry Ransom Center, University of Texas, Austin.

30   "**misunderstanding at any time about it**": 1948 Journal, Pierpont Morgan Library.

CHAPTER 5 · A JOURNAL,
THE TURTLE, AND INTERCHAPTERS

31   **"throbbing thing emerges"**: *WD*, 25.

31   **"too much of background"**: Ibid.

32   **"always had trouble with my work"**: JS to Mary, April 29, 1946, private collection.

33   **"best night for it"**: *WD*, 48.

33   **"approximately six pages a day"**: JS to Covici, June 1, 1938, Viking files.

35   **"Turtle sequence stands up"**: *WD*, 21.

35   **"satisfied this ambition of his"**: Mary Rodrigues, "This Is Steinbeck Country," *Monterey Peninsula Herald*, February 24, 1973.

35   **"sort of biblical"**: Bob Cathcart talk at Stanford Special Collections, 2000.

36   **"unless he were opened up"**: JS to Herbert Sturz, 1953, *New York Times*, August 6, 1990, A13.

36   **"reason for the movement"**: *WD*, 22, 23.

37   **"ashamed of selling things"**: Ibid., 28.

38   **"It is a significant difference"**: Edgar J. Hinkel and William E. McCann, eds., *Criticism of California Literature*, Alameda County Library, Oakland, Work Projects Administration, 1940, 854.

38   **"one feels it"**: Ibid., 857.

CHAPTER 6 · PARTICIPATION

39   **"thing in the world"**: ER Papers, Box 11, Stanford.

39   **"horizon clear"**: Post-Fire Journal III, Ed Ricketts Jr. Collection.

40   **"out into the world"**: Bruce Springsteen, "Bruce

Springsteen in Concert," *Bookmarks*, Summer 2002, San Mateo, CA, 21.

41   **"American Spirit"**: *AA*, 226.

42   **"good direction to be moved"**: Arthur Krim, "Here Comes That Rainbow Again," *Steinbeck Studies* 15 (2004): 133–36.

42   **"deep participation"**: ER, in Rodgers, ed., *Breaking Through*, 108.

43   **"minstrel rather than a scrivener"**: *LL*, 19.

43   **"one of my books"**: JS to Merle Armitage, February 17, 1939, Papers of John Steinbeck, MS 6239, Albert and Shirley Small Special Collections Library, University of Virginia.

44   **"the interchapters the refrain"**: Elaine Apthorp, "Steinbeck, Guthrie and Popular Culture," *San Jose Studies* 16 (1990): 19–39.

CHAPTER 7 · THIS "MIDDLEBROW" BOOK

45   **"middlebrow book"**: Leslie Fiedler, "Looking Back After 50 Years," *San Jose Studies* 16 (1990): 54–64.

47   **Gerald Haslam**: "*The Grapes of Wrath*: A Book That Stretched My Soul," in *The Other California: The Great Central Valley in Life and Letters* (Reno: University of Nevada Press, 1993).

47   **"white people were poor"**: Kay Levinson interview with author, May 16, 2013.

47   **"people not classes"**: JS to Albee, Bancroft Library, Berkeley.

48   **"over-essence of people"**: *WD*, 39.

50   **"explain and show them"**: Central Committee of the Arvin Camp to JS, Tom Collins letters, private collection.

50   **"lead pencils and lined paper as a torch for him"**:

Wilma Elizabeth McDaniel, www. back40publishing
.com/wembiblio.html.

51   "shame to our parents": JS to Beth, 1957, Wells
      Fargo Collection, Stanford.

51   "braver than I am": *WD*, 36.

52   "better than the one we have": JS 1939 radio script,
      JH Jackson Papers, Bancroft Library, Berkeley.

CHAPTER 8 · ISOLATOES AND THE GREATER WHOLE

53   "never yet melted": D. H. Lawrence, "Fenimore
      Cooper's Leatherstocking Novels," *Studies in Classic
      American Literature*, 1923, http://xroads.virginia
      .edu/~hyper/LAWRENCE/dhlcho5.htm.

56   "fine hater": *WD*, 24.

57   "recognized need": Glen A. Love, ed., *Practical
      Ecocriticism: Literature, Biology and the
      Environment* (Charlottesville: University of Virginia
      Press, 2003).

CHAPTER 9 · WRATH

60   "anger came up again": JS to Soule, Los Gatos,
      February 24, 1938, Pare Lorentz Papers, Pierpont
      Morgan Library.

62   "through newspapers": *LL*, 161–62.

62   "works of their hands and heads": JS, letter
      dated June 30, 1938, to John Barry. Printed in
      "Ways of the World," *San Francisco News*, July 13,
      1938, 14.

63   "literary people": JS to Lorentz, 1938, Pierpont
      Morgan Library.

65   **"healthiest thing in the world"**: JS,
     "Healthy Anger," *Books and Bookmen*, October
     1958, 24.

CHAPTER 10 · WOMAN TO WOMAN

66   **"She had a culture back of her"**: Helen Hosmer
     interview with Anne Loftis, February 24, 1983,
     author's files.
67   **"lives so alien to my own"**: Caroline Decker,
     interview with author, March 1989.

CHAPTER 11 · PICTURES

74   **"apparently unselected scenes"**: William Howarth,
     "Mother of Literature": Journalism and *The Grapes
     of Wrath*," in *New Essays on "The Grapes of Wrath,"*
     ed. David Wyatt (Cambridge, UK: Cambridge
     University Press, 1990), 71–99.
75   **"although done independently"**: JS to Covici,
     May 31, 1939, Viking files.
75   **"running comments for the book"**: Covici to JS,
     June 6, 1939, Viking files.
75   **"photographs . . . place of the activities"**: JS to TC,
     n.d., author's files.
75   **"collaborative text"**: Samantha Baskind, "The
     'True' Story: *Life* Magazine, Horace Bristol, and
     John Steinbeck's *The Grapes of Wrath*," *Steinbeck
     Studies* 15 (2004): 41–74.
76   **"make no mistake about it"**: Pare Lorentz, *FDR's
     Moviemaker: Memoirs and Scripts* (Reno: University
     of Nevada Press, 1992), 123.
76   **"anyone else"**: JS to Lorentz, 1938, Pierpont Morgan
     Library.

76 **"rather than people"**: Lozentz, *FDR's Moviemaker*, 43.

78 **"government's cooperation"**: Karel Ann Marling, *Wall-to-Wall America: Post Office Murals in the Great Depression* (Minneapolis: University of Minnesota Press, 2000), 31.

79 **"ability to write with a pen"**: "Wayward Bus" Journal, Pierpont Morgan Libary.

79 **"sit down on his haunches"**: Helen Hosmer interview with Anne Loftis, February 24, 1983.

CHAPTER 12 · "LOOSE AGGREGATIONS"

81 **"individual is paramount"**: ER, unpublished "Zoological Preface" to San Francisco intertidal book, 1939.

82 **"troubled time"**: Mitman, *The State of Nature*, 1.

82 **"fought the war"**: Carlton Sheffield, *Steinbeck: The Good Companion* (Portola Valley, CA: American Lives Endowment, 1983), 200–201.

85 **"farm laborers"**: Philip Bancroft, "The Farmer and the Communists," *Daily Commercial News*, San Francisco, April 29, 1935, 39.

85 **"Who Are the Associated Farmers?"**: Helen Hosmer, ed., "Who Are the Associated Farmers?" *The Rural Observer* (Simon J. Lubin Society of California) 1 (September–October 1938): 2–19.

CHAPTER 13 · THE SALINAS LETTUCE STRIKE, 1936

88 **"bent-over person was working"**: Hearings on short-handled hoe, National Steinbeck Center Archives.

89   **"spoiled, stupid, and arrogant"**: Carey McWilliams, "A Man, a Place, and a Time: John Steinbeck and the Long Agony of the Great Depression, Oppression, Frustration, and Hope," *American West* 7 (1970), 4–8.

90   **"embattled farmers"**: Lamb, "Industrial Relations," 1.

91   **"labor program"**: Ibid., 3.

91   **"the smoldering"**: *LL*, 132.

93   **"unforgivable thing I can think of"**: JS, "Conversation with Bo Beskow and Bo Holmstrom," August 12, 1962, Stanford.

93   *The California Report*: "Farmworker's Sexual Harassment Claim Leads to Trial, But Odds Are Long in Criminal Cases," *California Report*, June 28–30, 2013, http://www.californiareport.org/archive/R201306281630/d.

93   **don't know it exists**: Sasha Khokha, "Down on the Farm, Sexual Harassment Claims Finally Surface," July 24, 2008, http://www.californiareport.org/archive/R607240850/a.

CHAPTER 14 · HISTORY ON THE OUTSIDE

94   **"truly American book"**: *WD*, 29

95   **"new hope"**: Arthur Krim, "Elmer Hader and *The Grapes of Wrath* Book Jacket," *Steinbeck Newsletter* 4 (1991): 1–3.

98   **"subject matter more completely"**: Carol Steinbeck, JS, and Elizabeth Otis telegram to Covici, January 4, 1939, Columbia.

98   **"this book is a kind of march"**: LL, 171.

100   **"see it and feel it"**: JS to Elizabeth Otis, n.d., John Steinbeck Collection, Stanford.

101   **"face of intolerable wrong"**: Alicia Barnard

Thomsen, "Eric H. Thomsen and John Steinbeck,"
Steinbeck Newsletter 3 (1990): 1–3.

CHAPTER 15 · "THEY'S A LOT A FELLAS WANTA KNOW WHAT REDS IS."

103 **"a careful, meticulous observer"**: Frances Whitaker interview with author, February 1991.
105 **"leaving out any conclusion"**: *LL*, 99.
106 **"*Wizard of Oz*"**: Kazin, *American Dreamers*, 158.
106 **"is deeply devoted to his friends"**: Martin Ray, FBI file.
106 **"Do you know John Steinbeck?"**: Lorentz, *FDR Moviemaker*, 105–6.
107 **" environmental rescue"**: Kazin, *American Dreamers*, 277.

CHAPTER 16 · HISTORY ON THE INSIDE

112 **"law officials in California"**: http://articles.latimes.com/1986-02-02/opinion/op-3604_1_los-angeles-times.

CHAPTER 17 · MIGRANTS

115 **"farm labor in California"**: Carey McWilliams, "A Man, a Place and a Time," 4–8.

CHAPTER 18 · "CARE LIKE HELL"

119 **"without a hero and without a villain"**: Ella Winter and Granville Hicks, eds., *The Letters of Lincoln*

Steffens (New York: Harcourt, Brace and Company, 1938), 982.

121 **"tolerable in pigpens"**: Eric Thomsen, Bulletin #45, Associated Farmers, July 3, 1937.

122 **"difficult for them when they are here"**: Owens, *Trouble in the Promised Land*, 4.

122 **"every inch of the way"**: Helen Hosmer interview by Anne Loftis, February, 24, 1983.

123 **"and they aren't forever organizing"**: Charles L. Todd, "Trampling Out the Vintage," *Common Sense*, July 1939, 7–8, 30.

123 **"Comrade Iusi"**: "Suffering of Dust Bowl Era Recalled, *Monterey Herald*, August 4, 1989.

124 **"and a bed"**: *AA*, 215.

124 **"here at Kern"**: "Tom Collins reports," copies at CSS.

CHAPTER 19 · BEYOND THE JOAD NICHE

133 **"for this property"**: Celeste DeWald, "Interview with Victor Villaseñor," *Steinbeck Studies* 15 (2004): 129.

134 **"reestablished in the public mind"**: JS to Martin Luther King Jr., November 7, 1992, author's files.

135 **"quite like having something to say"**: Budd Schulberg, "John Steinbeck: Discontented Lion in Winter," *Los Angeles Times WEST*, February 23, 1969, 12–15.

137 **across cultures**: E. M. Loeb, *American Anthropologist*, 1929, 149, http://onlinelibrary.wiley.com/doi/10.1525/aa.1929.31.1.02a00150/pdf.

137 **Joseph Fontenrose**: *John Steinbeck: An Introduction and Interpretation* (New York: Barnes and Noble, 1963), 74.

CHAPTER 20 · SYSTEMIC SINS

141 "active church goer": Elaine Steinbeck interview with author, 1999.

141 "man plus his environment": JS, *To a God Unknown* ledger, Stanford.

141 "but that it doesn't die": *LL*, 221.

CHAPTER 21 · MA TO TOM: "EVER'THING YOU DO IS MORE'N YOU."

143 "whole story moves": *WD*, 36.

145 "as a whole": Covici to JS, January 9, 1939, Viking files.

145 "giving of a piece of bread": *LL*, 278.

145 "change in direction": Peter Miller, *The Smart Swarm: How Understanding Flocks, Schools, and Colonies Can Make Us Better at Communicating, Decision Making, and Getting Things Done* (New York: Avery, 2010), 29.

148 phenomenon of seed dispersal: Stephen Railton, "Pilgrims' Politics: Steinbeck's Art of Conversion," in *New Essays on "The Grapes of Wrath,"* ed. David Wyatt (New York: Cambridge University Press, 1990), 27–46.

CHAPTER 22 · RICKETTS ON *GRAPES*

151 "enlarged horizon of consciousness": ER to Evelyn Ott, June 30, 1938, ER Papers, Box 10, Stanford.

152 "these are varying in intensities of have to": ER Papers, Box 11, Stanford.

152 "of some sort, possibly 'becoming'": Ibid.

CHAPTER 23 · THE BOOK

154   **"thus corrupt Heaven. Love Pat"**: Covici to JS, telegram, February 26, 1948, Viking files.

155   **"frantic regard for my work"**: *LL*, 106.

155   **"I simply don't understand it"**: JS to F. B. Adams Jr., January 27, 1937, Pierpont Morgan Library.

156   **"no one forces any one to buy them"**: JS to Covici, Columbia University files.

157   **"most dignified publicity"**: February 14, 1939, Viking files.

157   **"no personality at all"**: *LL*, 180.

158   **"Send a postcard"**: "Viking's Guessing Contest on Steinbeck Shipments," *Publishers Weekly*, May 20, 1939.

159   **"attended Clark University"**: *Time Capsule, 1939* (New York: Time-Life Books, 1968), 200–202.

162   **"drawings for the book?"**: Covici to JS, August 2, 1939, Viking files.

162   **"of American illustration"**: Henry Adams, "Thomas Hart Benton's Illustrations for *The Grapes of Wrath*," *San Jose Studies* 16 (1990): 6–18.

163   **"left me in your debt"**: JS to Benton, April 13, 1964, misc. files, Benton Papers, Stanford.

163   **"satisfaction to be associated with it"**: Covici to JS, December 21, 1939, Viking files.

164   **Vietnamese, and Marathi:** List of translations provided by McIntosh and Otis.

164   **"should have been without him"**: *Pascal Covici, 1888–1964* (Meriden Gravure, 1964).

CHAPTER 24 · REACTIONS

166 "luck and destruction": *WD*, 6.

167 "'Grapes of Wrath'? Obscenity and Inaccuracy":
     "'*Grapes of Wrath*'? Obscenity and Inaccuracy,"
     Oklahoma City Times, May 4, 1939.

167 "portray[ing] life in such a bestial way": Karolides
     et al., *100 Banned Books*, 47.

168 "a line must be drawn somewhere": Bob Work,
     "Editorially Speaking," *Spartan Daily*, May 29,
     1939, 2.

168 "materials turned over to the La Follette
     Committee": JS to Carlton Sheffield, June 23, 1939,
     Good Companion.

170 "naked in the fields": Rick Wartzman, *Obscene in
     the Extreme: The Burning and Banning of John
     Steinbeck's* "The Grapes of Wrath" (New York:
     Public Affairs, 2008).

170 "presume to speak": Ibid., 210

CHAPTER 25 · DID *THE GRAPES OF WRATH* HELP THE MIGRANTS?

173 "La Follette Civil Liberties Committee": Helen
     Hosmer, ed., "Who Are the Associated Farmers,"
     The Rural Observer (Simon J. Lubin Society of
     California) 1 (September–October 1938): 2–19.

173 "dictatorship than part of the United States":
     Starr, 268–169.

174 "Be a good trick if I could": JS to Sheffield, January
     16, 1940, *Good Companion*.

174 "attached to a privy": Anne Lofis, "Steinbeck and the
     Federal Migrant Camps," *San Jose Studies* 16 (1990): 86.

CHAPTER 26 · THE FILM

176 **"believed my own story again"**: *AA*, 223.

177 **"not on the author"**: Nunnally Johnson, *The Letters of Nunnally Johnson,* eds. Dorris Johnson and Ellen Leventhal (New York: Alfred A. Knopf, 1981), 11.

178 **"director must try"**: John Ford, quoted in *The Grapes of Wrath*, Twentieth Century Fox Campaign Book, CSS.

179 **"*Grapes* as a social study"**: Ibid.

180 **"own words and your own songs"**: H. R. Stoneback, "Woody Sez: Woody Guthrie and *The Grapes of Wrath*," *Steinbeck Newsletter* 2 (1989): 8–9.

CHAPTER 27 · "NONE OF IT IS IMPORTANT OR ALL OF IT IS."

183 **"its timeless heart"**: Frank Rich, "New Era for 'Grapes of Wrath,'" *New York Times,* March 23, 1990.

184 **"concern for them"**: Jonathan Yardley, "A New Pressing of 'The Grapes of Wrath,'" *Washington Post Book World*, April 16, 1989, 2.

184 **"redeem us all"**: Alan Brinkley, "Why Steinbeck's Okies Speak to Us Today," *New York Times*, March 18, 1990, Arts 1, 12–13.

186 **"And I love them for it"**: JS to George Hedley, *Steinbeck Newsletter* 9 (1996): 16.

186 **"practical life, is what has made his life better"**: Robert DeMott, "Steinbeck on the Novel: A 1954 Interview," *Steinbeck Newsletter* 5 (1992), 6.

BIBLIOGRAPHY

◆ ◆ ◆

FOR THE PAST quarter century, I've been grateful that my star was hitched to this gracious, funny, empathetic, committed, and curious writer, a man whose company has never worn thin. Others, similarly smitten, have written appreciative essays and books on *The Grapes of Wrath*. I could not include them all. This bibliography contains only the material I reread, dipped into, and reconsidered in the past three months, when writing this book ever so quickly. Articles referenced in notes are not included in the bibliography. There are many fine critical studies of this novel that I do not mention, and I urge readers to consult Robert DeMott's excellent bibliography in the Penguin Classics edition of this novel.

Babb, Sanora. *Whose Names Are Unknown*. Norman: University of Oklahoma Press, 2004.

Beegel, Susan, Susan Shillinglaw, and Wesley N. Tiffney Jr. *Steinbeck and the Environment: Interdisciplinary Approaches*. Tuscaloosa: University of Alabama Press, 1997.

Benson, Jackson. " 'To Tom, Who Lived It': John Steinbeck and the Man from Weedpatch." *Journal of Modern Literature* 5 (1976): 151–94.

————. *The True Adventures of John Steinbeck, Writer.* New York: Viking, 1984.

Cassuto, David N. "Turning Wine into Water: Water as Privileged Signifier in *The Grapes of Wrath.*" In Beegel et al., *Steinbeck and the Environment,* 55–75.

Collins, Jennifer. "The Lingering Shadow: *The Grapes of Wrath* and Oklahoma Leaders in the Post-Depression Era." *Chronicles of Oklahoma,* Oklahoma Historical Society 81 (2003): 80–103.

DeMott, Robert. Introduction. In John Steinbeck, *The Grapes of Wrath.* New York: Penguin, 2006, ix–xlv.

Fender, Stephen. *Nature, Class, and New Deal Literature: The Country Poor in the Great Depression.* New York: Routledge, 2012.

French, Warren, ed. *A Companion to "The Grapes of Wrath."* New York: Penguin, 1989.

"Green Gold and Tear Gas: What Really Happened in the Salinas Lettuce Strike." *California: Magazine of Pacific Business,* November 1936.

Heavilin, Barbara A. *John Steinbeck's "The Grapes of Wrath": A Reference Guide*. Westport, CT: Greenwood Press, 2002.

Kappel, Tim. "Trampling Out the Vineyards—Kern County's Ban on *The Grapes of Wrath*." *California History* 61 (1982): 210–21.

Karolides, Nicholas, Margaret Bald, and Dawn B. Sova. *100 Banned Books*. New York: Checkmark Books, 1999.

Kazin, Michael. *American Dreamers: How the Left Changed a Nation*. New York: Knopf, 2011.

Lamb, Helen Boyden. "Industrial Relations in the Western Lettuce Industry." Ph.D. diss, Radcliffe College, 1942.

Madison, Charles A. "Covici: Steinbeck's Editor, Collaborator, and Conscience." *Saturday Review* 25 (June 1966): 15–16.

Mitman, Greg. *The State of Nature: Ecology, Community, and American Social Thought, 1900–1950*. Chicago: University of Chicago Press, 1992.

Owens, Louis. *"The Grapes of Wrath": Trouble in the Promised Land*. Boston: Twayne, 1989.

Owens, Louis, and Hector Torres. "Dialogic Structure and Levels of Discourse in Steinbeck's *The Grapes of Wrath*." *Arizona Quarterly* 45 (1989): 75–94.

Rodger, Katharine, ed. *Breaking Through: Essays, Journals, and Travelogues of Edward F. Ricketts*. Berkeley: University of California Press, 2006.

———. *Renaissance Man of Cannery Row: The Life and Letters of Edward F. Ricketts*. Tuscaloosa: University of Alabama Press, 2002.

Seelye, John. "Come Back to the Boxcar, Leslie Honey; or, Don't Cry for Me, Madonna, Just Pass the Milk: Steinbeck and Sentimentality." In *Beyond Boundaries: Rereading John Steinbeck*. Edited by Susan Shillinglaw and Kevin Hearle. Tuscaloosa: University of Alabama Press, 2002, 11–35.

Starr, Kevin. *Endangered Dreams: The Great Depression in California*. New York: Oxford University Press, 1996.

Steinbeck, John. *"America and Americans" and Selected Nonfiction*. Edited by Susan Shillinglaw and Jackson J. Benson. New York: Viking, 2002.

———. *The Forgotten Village: Life in a Mexican Village*. New York: Viking, 1941.

———. *A Life in Letters*. Edited by Elaine Steinbeck and Robert Wallston. New York: Viking, 1975.

———. *Working Days: The Journals of "The Grapes of Wrath."* Edited by Robert DeMott. New York: Penguin, 1989.

Steinbeck, John, and Edward Ricketts. *Sea of Cortez*. New York: Viking, 1941.

3 / 2014